Pioneer
Free Will Baptists
Ministers
Burial Locations
In
Tennessee

By

Dr. Alton E. Loveless

Copyright 2019
By
Dr. Alton E. Loveless

ISBN 9781523638482 Soft cover

2020 Update

This book was printed in the United States of America.

To order additional copies of this book, contact:
FWB Publications
Enchanting Acres
1006 Rayme Drive
Columbus, Ohio 43207
Alton.loveless@prodigy.net
Or
www.amazon.com

FWB
FWB Publications

Introduction

Tennessee

This book represents all that were part of the Free Will Baptist movement, consisting of the Palmer (south), Randall (north) and others such as the Stone, John-Thomas, John Wheeler Assns., NC OFWB and more.

Many of the photos are poor quality, but it was all I could find. Likewise, I do not have photos or tombstones for many of them. The information about these ministers were all that was available to me or found in archives. I made every effort to include those for which they would be remembered. Some I had no information, but research had shown they were of our denomination.

This Section is taken for a two Volume set done by this author.

Tennessee

James Richard Adams
Birth:
Unknown
Death:
Mar. 2, 2012
Antioch,
Davidson County, Tennessee
Burial:
Evergreen Cemetery,
Erwin, Unicoi County, Tennessee

Dr. Adams was born in Erwin, TN, and lived there until he moved to Nashville to attend Free Will Baptist Bible College. After graduating in 1966, Richard and his beloved wife Carolyn, moved to Kannapolis, NC, where he became the pastor of Ben Avenue Free Will Baptist and stayed until 1970. At that time, the couple, along with their two children moved to Elizabethton, Tennessee when

"Preacher Adams" served as the much-loved pastor of East Side Free Will Baptist Church for twenty years. In January of 1990, the Adams' family moved to Nashville, TN, where Richard became the Director of Development with Free Will Baptist Home Missions North America. Over the next eighteen years, Richard directed the Church Extension Loan Fund which enabled church planters to buy land and build facilities all across North America. Richard worked the Build My Church Campaign raising millions of dollars for Home Missions. He and Carolyn traveled around the world to Canada, Mexico, the Virgin Islands, Puerto Rico, and the United States, representing the cause of Christ and Home Missions. In honor of Richard's tireless work for missions, the Free Will Baptist Home Missions Board named the million-dollar endowment of funds he raised in his name-the Richard and Carolyn Adams Endowment. Dr. Adams made a tremendous impact of the cause of Christ and for Free Will Baptists around the world. He will be sorely missed not only by family, but also by literally hundreds of friends across our nation.

Randall Adkins
Birth:
Apr. 15, 1805
Tennessee
Death:

Aug. 16, 1888
Tennessee
Burial:
Adkins Cemetery, Oak Grove,
Campbell County, Tennessee

Broken Headstone Looks like the death date on stone could read August 6, 1888 but others have August 16, 1888.

W. S. Adkins
Birth:
Unknown
Death:
Mar. 25, 1904
Burial:
Adkins Cemetery, Oak Grove,
Campbell County, Tennessee

Member of Church for 15 years) age 51 years.

J A Albright
Birth:
Jun. 21, 1840
Death:
Nov. 30, 1921
Burial:
Albright Cemetery
Dickson County, Tennessee
He was one of the early Free Will Baptist ministers and central Tennessee and was affiliated with the Ashland Quarterly Meeting.

Rev Ephraim Wesley Akard
BIRTH
1858
DEATH
19 Mar 1934
BURIAL

Chuckey Community Cemetery
Chuckey,
Greene County,
Tennessee

He was on the list of those who showed JW Lucas and the unicoi college.

Hildon Clarence Beasley

Birth:
May 15, 1916
Stewart County, Tennessee
Dec. 21, 2003 Erin, Houston
County, Tennessee
Burial:
McIntosh Cemetery,
Houston County, Tennessee

He was a Free Will Baptist Minister.

Charlie Bennett
Birth:
Unknown
Death:
May 22, 2011
Johnson City
Washington County Tennessee
Burial:
Roselawn Memorial Park,
Johnson City,
Washington County, Tennessee

He was 93 at the time of his passing. He was a member and pastor of the True Gospel Free Will Baptist Church for nearly 50 years.

To be absent in body is to be present with the Lord

George Washington Binkley
Birth:
Oct. 17, 1850
Tennessee
Death:
Mar. 21, 1903
Davidson County,
Tennessee
Burial:
Turrentine-Binkley Cemetery
Ashland City
Cheatham County,
Tennessee

George Washington Binkley was the son of Turner and Martha (Mayo) Binkley. On Nov. 17, 1870,

Binkley married Florence Waggoner. In 1888 he was a member of the Ashland Quarterly Meeting in which he served as a Free Will Baptist minister.

James B Bloss
Birth:
1884
Death:
1959
Burial:
Polk MemorialGardens, Columbia, Maury County, Tennessee

Rev. J. O. Bloss, was a Free Will Baptist minister, affiliated and listed in the 1945 minutes of the National Ass'n.
In 1939, AL, he married Myrtle A (unk), and afterward they lived in Columbia, TN. where he was a pastor. He pastored in Tennessee and Alabama.
(WWI) Soldiers Grave Pearl Rivers. He was also a member of the Foreign Missions Board of the National Association.

To Die is the gain Him who gave life after death.

Rev Charles Dwight Bohanon
Birth:
Apr. 26, 1938
Death:
Jan. 9, 2015
Lancing, Tennessee
Burial:
Mount Hope Cemetery
Morgan County
Tennessee

His love for Christ lead him to be a Freewill Baptist Minister for over 40 years.
He was a loving husband to his wife Leila for 58 years, Loving father to 8 children, 19 grandchildren and 21 great-grandchildren. He was preceded in death by his parents, daughters, Marsha Lee, Mary Catherine, Son, and Charles Ricky

He is survived by his wife Leila Ellen Gallagher Bohanon, Daughters, Deborah (Rev. Henry) Miracle, Cynthia (Jon) Hankins, Kimberly Ellen (Gary) Crozier, Susan (John) Keathley, Son, Dwight (Michelle) Bohanon, 1 sister and 1 brother. Also surviving are a host of other family and friends. Rev. Henry Mircale, Rev. Joshua Crozier and Rev. Rick Taylor officiated.

Terry Lockert Boyd
Birth:
Unknown
Death:
Jan. 26, 2005
Pleasant View, Cheatham County, Tennessee
Burial:
Pleasant View Methodist Church Cemetery, Pleasant View, Cheatham County, Tennessee

A Free Will Baptist minister and owner of the Boyd Funeral Home in Ashland, Tennessee. He was a member of the Good Springs Free Will Baptist Church in Pleasant View, Tennessee. A book, *In My Father's Words*, was written by his daughter Sheila Boyd Cook in 2015 as a tribute to her father.

Fred L Bradshaw
Birth:
May 8, 1909
Death:
Mar. 5, 1963
Burial:
Highland Cemetery, Sparta, White County, Tennessee,

Fred Arvel Brewer
Birth:
Jul. 18, 1942
Johnson County,Tennessee
Death:
Apr. 20, 2002
Sullivan County, Tennessee
Burial:
Rainbow Cemetery Mountain City Johnson County, Tennessee

He was a Freewill Baptist Minister for 31 years. He had pastored several churches in Johnson City,

Washington County and Sullivan County. He sang with his family in churches all over North Carolina, Virginia and Tennessee.He was preceded in death by two brothers, Ernest Brewer and Rev. Bill Brewer.

William Lafayette Bright
Birth:
Jul. 4, 1883
Death:
Apr. 9, 1951
Burial:
Corinth Cemetery, Loudon, Loudon County, Tennessee

Rev Cicero A Brooks
Birth:
Jul. 18, 1854
Tennessee
Death:
Mar. 29, 1892
Tennessee
Burial:

Meadow Branch Cemetery
Bean Station
Grainger County
Tennessee

Rev. Cicero A. Brooks, son of P. M. and Sarah E. (Garrison) Brooks, married Nannie Holt in 1878, and has five children.

He was converted in 1879, two years later he received license, and Sept. 9, 1882, he was ordained. He devoted his time to teaching and preaching until 1885, when he entered upon revival work among the Free Baptist churches of eastern Tennessee and western North Carolina, which he has since continued with success, and some 200 being converted. He was the pastor of the Clear Creek church of the Union Association, Tennessee.

Rev Harley Cletis Brown
Birth:
May 15, 1922
Death
Nov. 18, 2014

Knoxville
Knox County
Tennessee
Burial:
Sherwood Memorial Gardens
Alcoa
Blount County, Tennessee

Retired pastor Harley C. Brown (92) of Knoxville, TN went to be with the Lord Tuesday, November 18, 2014. During his thirty year ministry, he pastored churches in Tennessee as well as four other states. He had been a longtime member of Forest Grove Free Will Baptist Church in Knoxville at the time of his death.

Board Valley
White County
Tennessee
Burial:
Board Valley Cemetery
Sparta
White County, Tennessee
An ordained Free Will Baptist minister whose name is found in old church records. The Rev G B "Dock" Brown, 78, pioneer Baptist minister, died at his Board Valley home after a lingering illness. Parents: Gideon Brown (1827 - 1880). Spouses: Lillie Clouse Brown (1883 - 1969) and Mary Vestina Stanley Brown (1858 - 1900).

Corp A H Burgess
Birth:
Apr. 17, 1844
Death:
May 14, 1922
Burial:
Liberty Freewill Baptist Church Cemetery,
Old Washington County,
Tennessee

He served in the 2nd NC Mounted Infantry Co E.

Rev Greene Baker Brown
Birth:
Jan. 23, 1857
Tennessee
Death:
Apr. 4, 1932

John Sankey Burgess
Birth:
Sep. 17, 1876
Tennessee
Death:
Jul. 3, 1952
Johnson City
Washington County
Tennessee
Burial:
Liberty Freewill Baptist Church
Cemetery Old
Washington County
Tennessee

A minister whose name appeared in 1938 Tenn. State Free Will Baptist minutes..

Rev Elmer Richard Carter, Sr
Birth:
May 30, 1927
Bristol
Sullivan County
Tennessee
Death:
Mar. 7, 2016
Mountain Home
Washington County
Tennessee
Burial:
Happy Valley Memorial Park
Elizabethton
Carter County
Tennessee

Reverend Elmer R. Carter, age 88, of Elizabethton, went home to be with the Lord from the James H. Quillen VA Medical Center Hospital. Reverend Carter was the son of Elmer Gaylord Carter and Maude Overbay Carter Stout. In addition to his parents, he was preceded in death by a son, Elmer Richard Carter, Jr.; and a sister, Betty Barlow.

Reverend Carter was born in Bristol, Tennessee but had lived most of his life in Carter County. He was a United States Navy veteran, having served in World War II. He was a retired minister and had served over 50 years in various Free Will Baptist churches. He was a member of East Side Free Will Baptist church and a member of Appalachian Association of Free Will Baptist, which he helped organize. He had also served as chairman of the board of Free Will Baptist Family Ministries. He had a passion for lost souls and loved his family and his church families.

A service to honor the life of Reverend Elmer R. Carter was conducted in the Riverside Chapel of Tetrick Funeral Home, Elizabethton with his son, Rev. David Carter, officiating and Rev. Justin Deaton, assisting.

Herman Christian
Birth:
Apr. 6, 1928
Death:
Jun. 9, 2008
Burial:
Center hill Cemetery,
Warren County, Tennessee

The idea is to die young as late as possible.

Benjamin Clouse
Birth:
Aug. 2, 1824
Cedar Creek
White County
Tennessee
Death:
Dec. 31, 1896
Board Valley
White County

Tennessee
Burial:
Board Valley Cemetery
Sparta
White County
Tennessee

His name appears in list of pioneer Free Will Baptist ministers in Putnam Co. Siblings: Benjamin Clouse (1824 - 1896)- John Clouse (1827 - 1897)- Francis Marion Clouse (1828 - 1892)- Nancy Ann Clouse (1832 - 1869)- William Riley Clouse (1835 - 1888)- Thomas Jefferson Clouse (1837 - 1895)- Elijah Crockett Clouse (1838 - 1908)- Charles Lee Clouse (1848 - 1917)- James Kelly Polk Clouse (1853 - 1921)- Simpson Clouse (1854 - 1913)- Andrew Jackson Clouse (1857 - 1913)- Dillard Martin Clouse (1866 - 1954)- Sarah Unicy *Clouse* Campbell (1869 - 1940).

Elder Thomas Jefferson Clouse, Sr
Birth:
Jan. 8, 1801
Washington County
Tennessee
Death:
Jul. 18, 1872
White County
Tennessee
Burial:
Thomas J. Clouse Cemetery
Monterey
Putnam County
Tennessee

Thomas Jefferson Clouse
Birth:
Jan. 1, 1837
Cedar Creek
White County, Tennessee
Death:
Nov. 11, 1895
Putnam County, Tennessee
Burial:
Clouse Cemetery
Cookeville
Putnam County, Tennessee

Thomas's occupation was a Preacher for Free-Will Baptist Church

Thomas was struck by a falling tree while clearing land. It crushed his chest and caused him to get pneumonia. He died a couple of weeks later. He died three months after his daughter, Rachel, was born of Peggy Eller. He was 71 years old.

Thomas married three times during his lifetime having many children and grandchildren.

Rev. T. J. Clouse, of Board Valley, died Monday night. He was taken violently ill Sunday and sank rapidly. Bro. Clouse was a most excellent gentleman and a good preacher. His presence will be greatly missed in his community. [Date 11/14/1895, Vol. IX, No. 3, Page 5]

The following church history was written by the late Judge Ernest Houston Boyd Sr. as part of a series of historical articles in the Putnam County Herald. It was published December 31,1953. The articles were compiled by Christine Spivey Jones into a book called Nuggets of Putnam County History.

The Free Union Baptist congregation is one of the oldest Baptist congregations in Putnam County. Its church building is located on the head of Martin's Creek, in the 18th District of Putnam County.

From 1865 until 1918 this was a Christian Baptist congregation, but since 1918 it has been affiliated with the Missionary Baptist denomination.

In the early history of the Free Union Church it was a large congregation, but on account of the building of other churches and the organization of new congregations in the section in which this church is located, its present membership is much smaller than it was in former years. This is also, partly due to deaths and removal from the community of a number of families active in this church in former years.

In its early history, when the congregation was a large one, the annual sessions of the Stone Christian Baptist Association were frequently held at this church. The old minutes of that Association show that both the 1891 and 1892 annual sessions of that Association were held with the Free Union Church. It seldom happen in the history of that Association that a second annual session of the Association, in succession, was held at the same church.

Among the early pastors of this church were T. J. Clouse, J. L. Kinnaird, F. M. Flatt, Benjamin Clouse, W. B. Gentry and J. W. Stone.

Thomas was ordained to preach in White County, Tennessee when a young man, and his life was spent as a Baptist Minister. Then came the Civil War. He was strongly opposed to slavery and often preached openly against it. In late December 1862, Thomas was holding a revival on the Calfkiller River. He was in the pulpit when the Guerillas came into the church and took him. They took him to Murfreesboro, arriving there December 31, 1862 at the Battle of the Stones River. He somehow managed to escape and made his way to the Union forces where he joined them. He worked in the hospitals and served as Union Army Chaplain throughout Kentucky and Ohio until the end of the war.

Inscription:
T.J. CLOUSE
BORN JAN 1, 1837
DIED NOV 11, 1895

Rev William Suttles Clouse
Birth:
Jan. 11, 1861
Board Valley
White County
Tennessee, USA
Death:
Dec. 9, 1943
Cookeville
Putnam County
Tennessee
Burial:
Cookeville City Cemetery
Cookeville
Putnam County, Tennessee

Rev. W.S. Clouse's name is listed in old Free Will Baptist minutes. He was in the Old Stone Association Minutes in 1879, when it convened in Cumberland Co., at Laurel Creek Church.

From the Book "*A Family History of Whitaker, Clours, Finley and Connected Families*" by Blanche Whitaker Jernigan: "William was a Baptist Minister like his father. He bought a tract of land on the Burgess Falls Road, which had been known as the Carmichael Farm in 1903. From J.V. Randolph he bought 27 acres, from J.M. Bray he bought 50 acres, and 20 acres from A.F. Massa all adjoining the Simp Officer line. He ran a grocery store there for many years. He later moved to Cookeville after he retired from the Ministry. He died in Cookeville on the 9th day of December 1943. William Suttle and his second wife Ann Eliza are buried at the Cookeville City Cemetery. His first wife is buried at the Broad Valley Cemetery in White County, Tennessee."

From the book "*A Book of Remembrance of The Clouse Family Descendants of George Clouse, I*" Compiled and Edited by Prietta Clouse Franklin Rt. 2 Box 408 Cookeville, Tennessee 38501:

"STINGING SERMON

Mrs. Estalee Rippetoe Howard of Cookeville relates the story of an old time country revival that reminds us of the one up home in years gone by when wasps to all intent and purpose broke up the service.

Mrs. Howard tells about a revival at the old Post Oak Shade Free Will Baptist Church. The house had no underpinning, she says, and every Tom, Dick and Harry's hogs slept under the floor. Which meant that fleas were hopping all over the place. Old Brother Sut Clouse was the evangelist and he was one of the big gun preachers, as the saying is back then. He really preached hellfire and damnation. He called himself the "Devil Skinner".

He would preach loud and pop his fists every few minutes. He could really make you think about things. I sang with the alto group and our seat was right near the front. But it was pretty hard to sing, or listen to the Word of God with a flea crawling up and down your spine, stopping every now and then to take a fresh bite.

I don't suppose hogs sleep under many churches any more to create a flea menace. But wasps still prefer a church to any other place to build their nests."

Thomas Charles Cofer

Birth:
Aug. 19, 1836
Death:
Aug. 10, 1885
Tennessee
Burial:
Carney Cemetery # 1
Whites Creek,
Davidson County, Tennessee

Thomas C. Cofer organized a Free Will Baptists church in 1880 at William T. Trotter's home. Trotter lived in a Civil War barracks on a dirt road, Buena Vista Pike. Pastor Cofer led in erecting a building at the corner of Buena Vista and Scott Street. He served as pastor of the church until his death in 1885.

The first Free Will Baptist church in Nashville, called the North Nashville Free Will Baptist Church, changed its name to honor the founder. That first building burned about ten years later and the city bought the lot for Buena Vista School on the street called Ninth Avenue North.

The church rebuilt on Arthur Avenue near what is now Garfield. In 1930 the congregation bought the brick building at 1600 Tenth Avenue North. The church built a parsonage there in 1952 for $8,000.

It was at this church that in 1935 the National Association of Free Will Baptists was formed through the efforts and leadership of the pastor of more than 40 years, John L Welch. Free Will Baptist Bible College in 2012 changed the name to Welch College in honor of him and his wife who had been a librarian and at the college for many years. He was also very influential in the early days of the college and very instrumental in it being in Nashville, Tennessee.

Cofer was married on May 14, 1857 to Florissa Moses who was born in 1836. Thomas was a Free Will Baptist preacher. They had the following children: William T.1858; James M. 1862; Sarah F. 1865; Johanna 1866; Charles M. 1869; David 1871; and Flora 1879.

Inscription:
Rev. T. C. Cofer
Born Aug. 19, 1836
Died Aug. 10, 1885
Blessed are the pure in heart for
they shall see God

Rev Frederick Cogswell

Birth:
Mar. 23, 1792
New Hampshire
Death:
Aug. 5, 1857
Memphis

Shelby County, Tennessee
Burial:
Elmwood Cemetery
Memphis
Shelby County, Tennessee
Plot: Lot 389, Chapel Hill

Frederick Cogswell, Free Baptist, son of Judge Thomas and Ruth (Badger) Cogswell, was born March 23, 1792. Labored in Barnstead, Allenstown, and other places in New Hampshire. In company with his cousin. Rev. Joseph Badger, and his brothers-in-law, Rev. John L. and Rev. Edward H. Peavy, he made preaching tours in the Southern and Western states and became a well-known preacher. Spent his later years, till 1853, in Tamworth. Residence, Memphis, Tenn., 1853-7. Died there, July, 1857.

Married Hannah Rogers, daughter of Col. Anthony and Elizabeth

Rev Charles Clifford Cooper
Birth:
Jun. 8, 1930
Rickman
Overton County
Tennessee
Death:
Apr. 6, 2016
Rickman
Overton County
Tennessee
Burial:
Okalona Cemetery
Okalona
Overton County
Tennessee

Rev. Charles Clifford Cooper, age 85, was born to the late George Cullum Cooper and Sarah Cooper Cooper.

Charles raised his family in Michigan and spent his adult life in the Ministry as a Free Will Baptist pastor. He was co-founder of three churches in Michigan; the East Side Free Will Baptist Church in Detroit, Faith Free Will Baptist in Romeo and the Free Will Baptist Mission in Lewiston, as well as helping his son establish the One-Eleven Fellowship in Cookeville Tennessee. During his time as pastor Bro. Cooper served two churches; the West Side Free Will Baptist Church of Detroit for 10 years and the Troy Free Will Baptist Church for 35. Charles also served on the Executive Committee of the National Association of Free Will Baptists, was the promotional director for the Michigan Association of Free Will Baptists, moderator of the Liberty Association of Free Will Baptists, and founder and editor of the Free Will Baptist monthly newspaper called the Menorah.

He enjoyed music and sang with the Tennessee Harmony Boys Trio for 10 years and the Straitway Trio for 14 years.

Bro. Cooper also had a radio ministry in Royal Oak, Michigan for 10 years. He enjoyed playing golf, and spending time with his grandchildren.

William Edward Coville, Sr
Birth:
Mar. 4, 1903
New York
Death:
Apr. 13, 1956
Madison
Davidson County
Tennessee
Burial:
Woodlawn Memorial Park and Mausoleum
Nashville
Davidson County, Tennessee

William E. Colville, d. from a sudden heart attack at age 54 yrs. He was the son of William Patrick COLVILLE, b. NY, and Phoebe (Ducette) COLVILLE, NY.

He was in armed services in 1920-22. In Tennessee he met and married Irene J. POLSTON, dau of Fred and Fannie POLSTON, Nashville, TN.

Wm. E. and Irene J. began their family in Nashville, where he worked in civil service as a postal clerk for R.R.

They were involved with her family in the Tennessee Free Will Baptist church work, where her mother was organizing and beginning a woman's auxiliary for the greater body. William E. served as Assistant Treasurer of the Eastern General Ass'n of FWB, in 1937 when it convened in So. Caroline, at Turbeville. They were living in Nashville, TN in the 1930.

Robert Barrett Crawford
Birth:
Jun. 21, 1913
Death:
Aug. 9, 2001
Burial:
Gibbs Cemetery, Ashland City, Cheatham County, Tennessee

A minister, denominational leader and the first full-time Executive-Secretary of the National Association of Free Will Baptists. He was converted to Christ at age 12, ordained to preach age 21, and pastored churches in Alabama, Tennessee, North Carolina and

Florida. He was the founding pastor of the Trinity Free Will Baptist Church in Greenville, North Carolina. He graduated from the University of Alabama and attended the Vanderbilt Divinity School. For 20 years he served in the Public Relations Department of Free Will Baptist Bible College in Nashville, Tennessee. He was active in ministry for 65 years and was one of the founders and shapers of the Free Will Baptist denomination.

Ronald Creech
Birth:
Unknown
Death:
Aug. 16, 2005
Burial:
Woodlawn Memorial Park,
Nashville,
Davidson County, Tennessee

A Free Will Baptist pastor, state Executive Secretary for the state of North Carolina Free Will Baptists. He retired from Free Will Baptist Bible College in Nashville Tennessee where he served as the Director Of Development.

Missionary Daniel Wickert Cronk
Birth:
February 28, 1923
Detroit Michigan
Death:
November 20, 1997
Nashville,
Davidson County, Tennessee
Burial:
Cremated

He graduated from Hazel Park High School, Detroit, Michigan; Free Will Baptist Bible College, Nashville, Tenn.; Columbia University, Columbia, South Carolina and Middle Tennessee State University, Tennessee. He was ordained to the gospel ministry in 1943 and served his denomination as a missionary to India for 25 years, a professor at Free Will Baptist Bible College for nine years and a member of the Board Of Foreign Missions for 15 years.

Missionary Trula *Gunter* Cronk

Birth:
Jun. 7, 1924
Greene County, Tennessee
Death:
Dec. 22, 2009,
Thailand
Burial:
Shelton Mission Cemetery,
Greystone,
Greene County, Tennessee

Mrs. Cronk grew up in the school years at Zion Mission, a circuit of schools and churches, which was started by the United Presbyterian missionaries from Pennsylvania.

She lived her teen years at Free Will Baptist Children's Home, located near Camp Creek School. Rev. I. L. and Mary Frances Stanley were very instrumental in her life. Later, the Rev. Paul and Nelle Woolsey would come to oversee the home and take Trula in as their own. She was the valedictorian of her graduating class at Camp Creek High School. With the love and support of "mom and dad" Woolsey, she was able to attend college and fulfill her calling to be a missionary to India. At the Free Will Baptist Bible College, in Nashville, where she would meet her future husband, Daniel Cronk, who was from Michigan. Together they went on to graduate from Columbia College in South Carolina. Trula also attended Peabody College. "They served the Lord as Free Will Baptist Pioneer Missionaries in India. The couple relocated to Nashville in 1972, where the Rev. Cronk was professor of the mission's program at the Free Will Baptist Bible College and Mrs. Cronk taught school in 1994. The home in which she lived at the Free Will Baptist Children's Home was given the name 'The Trula Gunter Cronk Home for Children' in honor of her being the first resident there. *"Over Mountain or Plain or Sea"* was published in 2003 and is a two-part autobiography detailing parts of Mrs. Cronk's childhood and her many years as a missionary. "In 2004, Mrs. Cronk moved back to Greeneville. Although she had lived in the Himalayas, traveled the Nile at midnight, seen the Taj Mahal, Buckingham Palace, the Louvre in Paris, Pharook's Palace in Alexandria, walked the Sahara Desert, climbed the Leaning Tower of Pisa and Cheops Pyramid, vacationed on beautiful Dal Lake in Sri Nafar, sipped tea with movie stars, world statesmen, and Scottish tea planters, shared seats with Mother Teresa, hunted crocodiles, tigers and rode camels, visited Japan, China, Germany, Russia and traveled the world over, no place was ever as dear to her as Greene County. In November of 2006, she left the mountains of East Tennessee to live with her son, Randall, a resident of Thailand.

Rev James Milton Crowson
Birth:
Mar. 15, 1930
Toccopola
Pontotoc County
Mississippi
Death:
Jun. 6, 2016
Nashville
Davidson County
Tennessee
Burial:

Woodlawn Memorial Park and Mausoleum
Nashville
Davidson County
Tennessee

James Milton Crowson was born the son of James Homer Crowson and Pearl Westmoreland Crowson. On April 9, 1949, he married Martha Frederick, whose father Joe Cephas Frederick pastored the church the Crowson family had begun to attend. He died peacefully in his sleep on June 6, 2016, at the age of 86. A history buff, he would have appreciated the significance of passing away on the day of the WWII allied invasion of Normandy, known as D-¬Day.
In 1955 he moved his young family to Nashville, TN, where he began his B.A. program at Welch College (known then as Free Will Baptist Bible College). He managed to keep up a full academic load, and support a family, all while working as a tool and die maker, usually the night shift. Following graduation in 1960, he began studies for his M.A. at Bob Jones University. He completed his degree after having served as pastor to churches in South Carolina, Oak Ridge, Tennessee, and Russellville, Alabama. In 1968 he moved back to Nashville to join the faculty of Welch College. It was not, however, his first experience as a Welch College instructor. In his senior year, he had been asked to step in temporarily to teach beginning Greek for the normal

professor, Dr. Robert Picirilli, who was continuing his own studies at the time!

Later, he worked again as a tool and die maker, wallpaper tradesman, as well as a condo-apartment property manager.

Milton Crowson loved God, the Bible, his wife, his family, history, gardening, and fishing — and usually in that order, although history and fishing often tried to move higher up the list!.

Rev Matthew F Curtis
Birth:
Oct. 11, 1849
Caplin, Tennessee
Death:
Apr. 22, 1923
Dowelltown
DeKalb County,
Tennessee
Burial:
Snow Hill Baptist Church Cemetery
Smithville
DeKalb County,
Tennessee

He was converted in 1865 and two years later received license to preach from the Methodist Episcopal denomination.

He was ordained in September, 1878, by the new union association and conducted several revival and organized four churches and was engaged in publishing the Christian Progress and was a manager for a company for printing religious tracts in 1889. He took a leading

position in the New Union Conference.

Matthew first married Mary Elizabeth Johnson in 1867. After her death he married Louvisa Jane Vanderpool in 1880. After her death he married Lillie Scurlock in 1913.

Robert M Cutshall
Birth:
Aug. 23, 1912
Death:
Dec. 10, 1990
Burial:
Burnetts Chapel Cemetery,
Greene County, Tennessee

James Thomas Davis

Birth:
Unknown
Death:
Aug. 11, 2001
Burial:
Williamson Memorial Gardens,
Franklin,
Williamson County, Tennessee

Dr. Davis was a minister, church planter, pastor, professor and research scientist. He was a founder of a number of churches in central Tennessee and at his retirement was pastor emeritus of the Franklin Community Church. He had been a professor at Free Will Baptist Bible College and was a Bio-Chemist with the Vanderbilt University Medical School.

Rev. N.N. Jennings "Bud" Dotson

Born:
April 14, 1943
Dickenson County, Virginia
Death:
December 7, 2019

Kingsport, Tennessee
Burial:
Unknown

He was born to Nade and Rosa Mae Dotson. After graduating from the American College of Life Underwriters, he would become a district manager with People's Life Insurance Company, Washington, D.C. While in the nation's capital, Jennings met his wife, Ruth, at the introduction of their mutual friends. They were soon married on December 26, 1963 and began their lives together. Before retiring to Kingsport, Jennings and Ruth made their home in Alexandria, Roanoke, Lynchburg, Church Road, and Bristol, Virginia.

Although Jennings was raised in church, it was not until the winter of 1965 that he put his faith in Christ and was baptized along with his wife. He was called to preach the gospel in 1973, and bi-vocationally pastored several churches: Chestnut Hill Free Will Baptist Church (Big Island, VA), Lighthouse Free Will Baptist Church (Petersburg, VA), Cornerstone Free Will Baptist Church (Bristol, TN), and Genesis Free Will Baptist Church (Kingsport, TN).

Preacher Dotson loved southern gospel music, especially by such greats as J.D. Sumner & the Stamps. It was that love that led him to become the owner/operator of Sunshine Broadcasters Inc./WBCV Christian Radio in Bristol, as well as the host of two syndicated programs: Gospel Gold and Harvest Time. Dotson involved himself in community, coaching youth league sports, participating in the Virginia High School Band Boosters, and serving as the chairman of the board for the Duffield, VA-based Harvest Child Care Ministries for nearly 30 years.

Many only knew Dotson by his radio voice, but those who knew him best describe Jennings as a true blessing, a godly Christian, and a strong general in God's army. Even during his own illness, he demonstrated compassion for others by visiting hospitals, nursing homes, and by phone. His sons recount his strong work ethic and love for Christ's church as an example for their own ministries. Rev. Dotson is survived by his two sons, Deacon Newl Dotson of Kingsport and Pastor Chris Dotson of Morristown.

F. A. Dewitt
Birth:
Mar. 9, 1883
Death:
May 21, 1970
Burial:
McMinn Memory Gardens,
Athens,
McMinn County,
Tennessee

Robert H Doan
Birth:
Mar. 25, 1907
Virginia
Death:
Nov. 9, 2001
Medina County, Ohio
Burial:
Morning View Cemetery
Bluff City
Sullivan County, Tennessee

Early Free Will Baptist pastor who served in West Virginia pastoring the Ansted Free Will Baptist Church in 1955-56. He also spent time in Ohio.

George D. Dunbar
Birth:
Aug. 13, 1889
Tennessee
Death:
Jun. 20, 1968
Washington County,
Tennessee
Burial:
Liberty Freewill Baptist Church
Cemetery,
Old Washington Cty,
Tennessee

George Dobson Dunbar In June 1917, registered for WW I Draft. He was described as tall and of medium build, blue eyes and brown hair. He was a minister in the Free Will Baptist Church where he was ordained, and became a leader in the eastern Tennessee Free Will Baptist churches. He was Pastor, Evangelist and Exec. Sec'y of the Union FWB Assn., in Washington Co. in the 1940's.

He was responsible for the preparation, arrangement and publication of *"God, A Hundred Years and A Free Will Baptist Family"* by Rev. Paul Woolsey, a FWB Missionary to India, a book which preserved many historical facts and accounts that could have been lost had it not been published.

Zadock D. Duncan
Birth:
Feb. 1, 1830
Death:
Feb. 1, 1921
Burial:
Hoodoo Cemetery
Hoodoo
Coffee County, Tennessee

He was a Free Will Baptist minister affiliated with the New Union Association which belong to the state of Tennessee. He served in the Military - Lt, Co., I, 34th TN Infantry, C.S.A

Kenneth Paul Eagleton
Birth:
Jul. 1, 1928
Death:
Aug. 26, 1999
Burial:
Middle Tennessee State Veterans Cemetery,
Nashville,
Davidson County,
Tennessee, Plot: PP 02 15

Minister, missionary to Brazil for International Missions of the Free Will Baptist denomination. He was a graduate of Free Will Baptist Bible College in Nashville, Tennessee. He was a veteran of the United States Air Force and achieved the rank of staff Sgt. and served in Korea.

Missionary Marvis Eagleton
Birth:
Apr. 27, 1926
Death:
Feb. 21, 2003
Burial:
Middle Tennessee State Veterans Cemetery, Nashville, Davidson County, Tennessee, Plot: PP 02 15

She was a missionary to Brazil for the International Board of Foreign Missions for the Free Fill Baptist denomination. She was a graduate of Free Fill Baptist Bible College in Nashville, Tennessee.

William Donald Ellis
Birth:
2 Jan 1931
Montgomery County,
Tennessee
Death:
1 Jan 2018
Fairfield,
Freestone County,
Texas
Burial:
Heads Free Will Baptist Church
Cemetery
Cedar Hill,
Robertson County,
Tennessee,

William Donald Ellis, 87, of Fairfield, TX formerly of Longview, TX, at his daughter's home in Fairfield. He was born, in Montgomery County, TN to the late William Robert and Alice Gertrude Gower Ellis. He graduated from Coopertown High School in Coopertown, TN with the class of 1949, and attended Freewill Baptist Bible College in Nashville, TN and served as a minister his entire life. He married Emma Elizabeth Johnson on Sept.

4, and she preceded him in death on Feb. 16, 2000. Mr. Ellis moved to Fairfield three years ago from Longview. He was a member of First Freewill Baptist Church in Carthage. Mr. Ellis was preceded in death by his parents; wife; brother, Bobby Ray Ellis; and son, Donald Jewel Ellis.

A funeral service, at Jimerson-Lipsey Funeral Home Chapel with Bro. Mike Fields and Bro. Shane King officiating.

Herman Hughes Ellis
Birth:
Jul. 2, 1934
Gause, Tennessee
Death:
Jul. 19, 2006
Cedar Hill, Tennessee
Burial:
Heads Free Will Baptist Church
Cemetery,
Cedar Hill,
Robertson County, Tennessee

He was saved in July of 1960, and later attended the Free Will Baptist Bible College and ordained as a Minister of the gospel at Head's Free Will Baptist Church in 1961.

He was a pastor in Michigan, Alabama and Tennessee and used as an evangelist across the entire nation.

George W. Farless
Birth:
Apr. 15, 1885
Death:
Apr. 24, 1968
Burial:
Gnat Hill Cemetery
Manchester
Coffee County, Tennessee

He was a minister in the New Union Association of Free Will Baptists.

Harrison William Farrell
Birth:
Jan. 15, 1848
Coffee County,
Tennessee
Death:
Aug. 6, 1924
Warren County,
Tennessee
Burial:
Hillsboro Cumberland
Presbyterian Cemetery
Hillsboro
Coffee County,
Tennessee

He was a minister that was affiliated with the new Union Association, which had been affiliated with the United Baptists, and the state of Tennessee

Winford R Floyd
Birth:
1932
Death:
1995
Burial:
Happy Valley Memorial Park,
Elizabethton,

Carter County, Tennessee, Plot: Mausoleum of Peace

He was a well-known Minister in eastern Tennessee and active in denominational leadership.

Joe T Fort
Birth:
Dec. 27, 1866
Death:
May 22, 1924
Burial:
Fort Family Cemetery,
Clarksville,
Montgomery County, Tennessee

Edward Johnson Fox
Birth:
23 Dec 1933
Tennessee
Death:
26 Nov 2017
Tennessee
Burial:
Greenbrier Cemetery
Franklin,
Williamson County, Tennessee

He always had a smile on his face. He worked for his company, Fox Insurance Agency, and served his community for ovRead More er 30 years. He was extremely active in his community and enjoyed being the Pastor at Berean Freewill Baptist Church. He loved people and he was loved by everyone.

Estel M French
Birth:
Sep. 12, 1902
Death:
Apr. 21, 1978
Burial:
Mosheim Central Cemetery,
Mosheim, Greene County,
Tennessee

Jake Muriel French
Birth:
Dec. 7, 1901
Death:
Oct. 7, 1966
Burial:
Hickory Valley Cemetery
Unitia
Loudon County
Tennessee

Wooley's book mentions him at the FWB Home for children.

Malcolm Craig Fry
Birth:
Jun. 6, 1928
Detroit,
Wayne County, Michigan
Death:
Aug. 24, 2007

Locust Grove,
Mayes County,
Oklahoma
Burial:
Hermitage Memorial Gardens,
Old Hickory,
Davidson County,
Tennessee

He was a Free Will Baptist minister and a denominational leader. He was the National Church Training Service Director and Adult Curriculum Director at Randall House in Nashville Tennessee. He was an outstanding pianist and singer and made many recordings. He also served with the U.S. Army and was also a U.S. Air Force Veteran;

You Are Home At Last!

Willie M. "Bill" Gardner, Jr
Birth:
Unknown
Norfolk,
Norfolk City, Virginia
Death:
Jun. 15, 2001
Nashville,
Davidson County, Tennessee
Burial:
Woodlawn Memorial Park,
Nashville,
Davidson County, Tennessee

A well-known pastor, recording artist and denominational leader whose singing ability brought many pulpit opportunities. During his ministry, he pastored churches in four states; Tennessee, Indiana, Mississippi and Georgia. He attended Free Will Baptist Bible College, with later studies at North Carolina State University, and earned a master's degree in music at Mississippi State University. He was known for his clear, high tenor voice singing frequently at many national conventions, state associations and Bible conferences. He was a member of the Music Commission and Media Commission. His last recording effort occurred during the production of *"He Keeps Me Singing"* video which featured 50 Free Will Baptist singers and musicians. He was a role model for many musicians and singers.

Benjamin F Garland
Birth:
1846
Death:
September 15, 1887
Burial:
Garland Cemetery
Carter County,
Tennessee

He was a Free Will Baptist minister and died at age 35. The Headstones Provided for Union Soldiers.

Inscription:
Co L, 13th Tenn Cav.

Rev Vernon Hugo Gober
Birth: Jun. 7, 1938
Winston County
Alabama
Death: Jul. 28, 2004
Adamsville
McNairy County, Tennessee
Burial:
Milledgeville Cemetery
Milledgeville
McNairy County, Tennessee

REV. VERNON H. GOBER of Adamsville, 66, was born AL the son of Victor Hugo and Mattie

Naomi Owen Gober. He was united in marriage to the former O. Ruthie Benson on Aug. 16, 1961. Rev. Gober was a Free Will Baptist minister for 40 years and a farmer. He pastored churches in Tennessee and Alabama. He was a member of Plummer's Chapel Free Will Baptist Church and served on the board of directors for the Free Will Baptist Family Ministries in Greeneville. He was a former member of Soil Conservation and McNairy Farmers CO-OP. He was a veteran of the United States Navy. Dr. James Kilgore, Dr. Charles Thigpen and Rev. James Carrington officiated.

H. Wilks Gower

Birth:
Aug. 3, 1842
Death:
Feb. 5, 1924
Burial:
Heads Free Will Baptist Church Cemetery, Cedar Hill
Robertson County, Tennessee

James W Gower

Birth:
Aug. 30, 1821
Robertson County, Tennessee
Death:
Jul. 29, 1886
Robertson County, Tennessee
Burial:
Heads Free Will Baptist Church Cemetery
,Cedar Hill,
Robertson County, Tennessee

Was a minister in the Free Will Baptist Church for 29 yr. (written on tombstone.

Paul Frederick Hall

Birth:
Feb. 20, 1938
Durham, Durham County, North Carolina
Death:
Nov. 5, 2008
Nashville, Davidson County, Tennessee
Burial:
Spring Hill Cemetery, Nashville, Davidson County, Tennessee

He graduated from Durham High School in 1956, That fall he entered FWBBC. After attending two years he married Ruthann Edwards from Illinois in August 1958. Fred was called as assistant pastor at Swannanoa FWB church. During that time their first child was born. The family returned to Nashville to continue his education. After another year of college, Fred was called to be minister of music and assistant pastor at Central FWB church in Royal Oak, Michigan.. After two years the desire to finish his education led Fred to resign and return to Nashville. Finally in 1964 he received his BA degree. Fred served churches in North Carolina, South Carolina, Tennessee, Illinois, Kentucky and Michigan during his years of ministry. Fred wrote Sunday School literature for Randall House Publications several years and served in several roles in the denomination. Many people knew him for his beautiful singing voice and while he loved to sing, his first love was preaching and teaching. In 1984 Fred earned a Master of Arts Degree in Pastoral Studies from FWBBC. In 2000 he earned a second Master's degree from this Pensacola Christian Seminary in Bible Exposition.

health was failing and was not able to attain that goal. He loved to study and maintained a 4.0 grade average in both of his masters programs. During his lifetime Fred had built up quite a library. When he passed away, his family gave it to Trinity FWB Church in Bowling Green, KY. The "Rev. Fred Hall Memorial Library" was established in his honor. They had celebrated their 50th wedding anniversary on August 17 of that year while he was in the hospital.

He had started work on a doctor's degree from Pensacola Christian Seminary, but by this time his

Charles Edgar Hampton
Birth:
Mar. 25, 1938
Blanchard,
McClain County, Oklahoma
Death:

Mar. 5, 2007
Nashville,
Davidson County, Tennessee
Burial:
Harpeth Hills Memory Gardens,
Nashville,
Davidson County, Tennessee

Dr Hampton is an alumnus of Free Will Baptist Bible College, Oklahoma Baptist University, Oklahoma University, and the University of Texas. He also retired from the Free Will Baptist Bible College after 26 years. Funeral services was at the Free Will Baptist Bible College with Dr Paul Harrison officiating.

Ralph C. Hampton
Birth:
Dec. 13, 1934
Dibble, McClain County, Oklahoma
Death:
Sep. 7, 2012
Nashville. Davidson County.

Tennessee
Burial:
Harpeth Hills Memory Gardens,
Nashville,
Davidson County, Tennessee

The Oklahoma native was converted at age 12 during a youth camp and ordained to preach in 1960. Hampton's ministry to the broader denomination included six pastorates in Tennessee and Missouri, articles for *Contact* and *ONE Magazine,* and curriculum writing for Randall House Publications. His signature leadership role came during a 15-year span when the National Association of Free Will Baptists elected him moderator nine times (1987-1996) and assistant moderator six times (1981-1987). He moderated during several controversial and pivotal sessions, including the emotionally charged 1995 national convention. Ralph began his 50-year tenure at Welch College in 1958 at age 23. Like most young educators, he wore several hats, which meant that he taught 15 hours per semester, served as Christian Service Director, and was the dormitory supervisor. The son of a Free Will Baptist preacher and oldest of four brothers, he spent half a century changing the landscape of denominational education, preparing students for ministry in a world-wide community, and raising a family of three children with his wife Margaret—all three children graduated from Welch College. He pushed himself hard as an educator, earning five degrees — A.A. degree from East Contra Costa Junior College (1955), B.A. degree from Welch College (1958), M.A. degree from Winona Lake School of Theology (1961), M.Div. from Covenant Theological Seminary (1970), and the D.Min. (ABD) from Trinity Evangelical Divinity School. He was the former chairman of the Biblical and Ministry Studies Department at Welch College and a member of the college faculty for 50 years, died after a two-year battle with cancer.

R S Harris
Birth:
1870
Death:
1940
Burial:
Troy Cemetery
Troy
Obion County,
Tennessee

He was a member of the Clinch River Association which was situated west of the John Wheeler Association in Virginia and Tennessee.

And was one of the early ministers the Association.

Rev. Harrold Harrison
Birth:
1925
Henryetta, Oklahoma
Death:
July 11, 2019
Nashville, Tennessee

Harrold D. Harrison, 94, was predeceased by his wife of 71 years Lauretta; his parents Eugene and Mabel Harrison; and six brothers and one sister.

He is survived by his daughter Marilyn Smith of Nashville; three sons, David and wife Eileen of Lincoln Park, MI, Paul and wife Diane of Huntsville, AL, and Jeff and wife Sallie of Prague, OK; grandchildren, Carrie Willis, Monica, Andrew, Adam, Ashley, Justin, and William Harrison; great-grandchildren, Anneliese Evans, Charlie, Lucy and Matthew Harrison and Gabriel McKenzie; three sisters and many nieces and nephews.

Harrold received his B.A. from Welch College and M.A. from Middle Tennessee State University.

After several years of ministry as a pastor in Free Will Baptist churches, he worked for their National Sunday School Department, Randall House Publishers and Welch College. Harrold served in the Navy during World War II and never forgot those years and his experiences in the Pacific aboard the battleship U.S.S. Maryland. His war stories were fascinating and full of detail.

To know Harrold or even just to meet him was to know that he was a Christian. He lived and practiced his faith daily with joy and gratitude and made a positive difference in the lives of so many. Harrold's life was celebrated in a service at Cross Timbers Free Will Baptist Church..

Greenbrier Cemetery, Greenbrier
Robertson County, Tennessee
A Free Will Baptist pastor for 25 years serving five churches in Michigan, Tennessee, Florida and Georgia. He was a prolific writer and noted historian serving 10 years on the National Historical Commission. He launched *"The Time Machine"* for the Georgia FWB Historical Society and *"Resources for Free Will Baptist History"* for the national commission. He researched and wrote a 35 chapter historical novel about the denomination which was in its final stages when he died.

Wallace Ray Hayes
Birth:
Jun. 21, 1940
Tennessee
Death:
Sep. 24, 2015
Mount Juliet
Wilson County, Tennessee
Burial:
Greenwood Cemetery
Charlotte
Dickson County, Tennessee

Steven Robert Hasty
Birth:
Jun. 15, 1949
Death:
Apr. 21, 1998
Tennessee
Burial:

Mr. Hayes was a Freewill Baptist Minister who has served in Davidson, Dickson, Humphreys, Stewart & Wilson counties. He was very devoted and worked very closely with the Cumberland Youth Camp for over 45 years.

George Head
Birth:
Mar. 14, 1794
Death:
Oct. 27, 1868
Burial:
Heads Free Will Baptist Church
Cemetery
Cedar Hill
Robertson County
Tennessee

A pioneer in the church work for Free Will Baptists in Tennessee. He was baptized by Rev. Robert Heaton, another early minister. He gave 1/2 acre for the cemetery.

Rev George R Head
Birth:
Aug. 4, 1834
Robertson Co Tennessee
Death:
Jul. 5, 1902
Burial:
Heads Free Will Baptist Church
Cemetery
Cedar Hill
Robertson County
Tennessee

Rev. George Richard HEAD, son of George and Elizabeth (Winters) HEAD, At the age of nineteen he was converted, and July 14, 1866, he received a license. The following year he was ordained [Free Will Baptist minister]. His ministry has been in the Cumberland Association, TN, in which he has occupied a prominent position. He was married to Joanna F. Moore, October 23, 1853."

Rev George Richard Head
Birth:
Apr. 6, 1857
Death:
Dec. 31, 1927
Burial:
Heads Free Will Baptist Church
Cemetery
Cedar Hill
Robertson County
Tennessee

Free Will Baptist minister in the latter 1800's until his death.

Was married to Lavina Ann (Harris)...sometimes listed as Ann, or Anna Lavina.

Children: Hubert Head (1888 - 1943), Ernest Head (1893 - 1982)

Rev Wiley H Head
Birth:
Jan. 27, 1818
Death:
Apr. 5, 1888
Burial:
Heads Free Will Baptist Church
Cemetery
Cedar Hill
Robertson County, Tennessee

Rev. W.H. Head, listed in FWBapt Cyclopedia as "prominent minister having died recently." [pub. 1889]. He served among the Ashland Quarterly Meeting, TN.

He was an early Free Will Baptist minister in the Ashland Quarterly Meeting, whose name appears in a listing of churches and pastors: Good Spring; Heads; Bethlehem; Oakland; Charity; Mt. Zion; Shady Grove; Grange; Old Zion; Oaklawn and North Nashville. Rev. W. H. Head was a minister of one of those churches, maybe, more than one as the custom was in that early day. Parents: George Head (1794 - 1868) & Elizabeth Winters Head (1800 - 1856). Spouse: Angaline D Head (1858 - 1890). Sibling: George R Head (1834 - 1902).

Robert Heaton
BIRTH
15 Mar 1765
Augusta County, Virginia, USA
DEATH
15 Nov 1843 (aged 78)
Ashland City, Cheatham County,
Tennessee, USA
BURIAL
Forest Hill Cemetery
Ashland City, Cheatham County,
Tennessee

A minister of the Gospel in early Tenn.

William H. Head
Birth:
Mar. 31, 1839
Death:
Jul. 10, 1923
Burial:
Heads Free Will Baptist Church
Cemetery,
Cedar Hill,
Robertson County, Tennessee

Herman Lawrence Hersey
Birth:
Jan. 1, 1926
Chicago,
Cook County, Illinois
Death:
Jan. 26, 2008
Jackson,
Madison County, Tennessee
Burial:
Highland Memorial Gardens
Jackson
Jackson County, Tennessee

A Free Will Baptist minister, pastor and denominational executive. A minister of the gospel for 58 years serving churches in North Carolina and was the Director of the Board of Retirement and Insurance for the National Association Of Free Will Baptists. He was a graduate of Bob Jones University, Chicago Musical College and attended the St. Louis Institute of Music at George Washington University. He is remembered as an outstanding pianist.

Rev. Bud Hill
Birth:
May 4, 1934
St. Louis, Missouri
Death:
May 24, 2019
Pleasant View, Tennessee
Burial:
EverRest
Cheatham, Tennessee

Mr. Hill was born to the late Chesley and Nellie Mae Irene Hughes Hill. He served and preached for over 65 years in many churches among the Free Will Baptist denomination. He also taught school for 30 years and was an avid supporter of Welch College. He was a member of the Heads Free Will Baptist Church.

William J. Hill
Birth:
Jan. 10, 1928
Death:
Aug. 17, 2001
Burial:
Green Acres Memorial Gardens, Crossville, Cumberland County, Tennessee

Hill was a Minister that span 50 years and was the college chaplain at Taylor University in Indiana. He spoke in many universities in the United States as well as abroad. He began his ministry in 1948 as Minister of the first Free Will Baptist Church in Myrtle, Missouri.

Later he pastored churches in Tennessee and Michigan and later the Evangelical Mennonite church in Indiana and Ohio. He was a graduate of the Free Will Baptist Bible College in Nashville and did graduate work at the University of Detroit in Michigan and Anderson College in Indiana.

And was author Of "Organizing The Free Will Baptist Sunday School" printed by Randall house publications. Two other brothers were also noted ministers, namely; Bob Hill and Dr. Don Hill.

Rev Glenn L. Hoilman
Birth
23 Mar 1940
Burnsville, Yancey County,
North Carolina
Death
13 May 2018
Elizabethton, Carter County,
Tennessee
Burial
Piney Flats United
Methodist Church Cemetery Piney
Flats, Sullivan County, Tennessee

Rev. Glenn L. Hoilman, 78, Watauga went in the Sycamore Shoals Hospital after an extended illness.

A native of Burnsville, North Carolina, he was a son of the late Millard Filmore Blonda Grindstaff Hoilman.

He was a retired Mechanic. Rev. Hoilman had served as a pastor for over 42 years. He pastored Y Free Will Baptist Church for 30 years. He was a member of True Gospel Baptist Church, Elizabethton. Funeral Services in Memorial Funeral Chapel with the Rev. Dean Presnell and Dexter Hoilman officiating.

Critt Holman
Birth:
Sep. 6, 1908
Death:
Sep. 27, 2002
Burial:
Stewart Cemetery,
Cookeville,
Putnam County, Tennessee

James T Holman

Birth

1887

Death

1956 (Aged 68–69)

Burial

Evergreen Cemetery
Murfreesboro, Rutherford
County, Tennessee, Usa

Nathan Honeycutt

Birth:

Jul. 20, 1824
Buncombe County,
North Carolina

Death:

1907

Burial:
Nathan Honeycutt Cemetery,
Tiger Valley,
Carter County, Tennessee

Nathan was an early Free Will Baptist minister and was noted in Paul H. Woolsey's *"My Woolsey Free Will Baptist Family"*, pub. 1949:"Reverends Nathan Honeycutt and "Bobby" Moore's labors were especially blessed in Carter County, Tennessee. Today (1949) there are more Free Will Baptist Churches in this than any other county in the state - some twenty, belonging to the Union and Toe River Associations. Brother Honeycutt was the first minister to enter the young association after its birth in 1850. Of all the other early leaders, Brother Honeycutt proved to be the most earnest and efficient helper, outside the Union Association, in the planning and building of a denominational school. Soon after commencement of Free Will Baptist work in this vicinity Father Woolsey began correspondence with the General Conference of the North. It was Brother Honeycutt who stood with him for the unification of the work with the entire denomination. In those formative years many questions of policy, doctrine and rules had to be adopted. "His ability and leadership was instrumental to the church's growth in that part of Tennessee.

Joseph Clarence Howington
Birth:
Aug. 27, 1889
Death:
Jul. 20, 1970
Burial:
Highland Cemetery
Elizabethton
Carter County, Tennessee

Mentioned in 1937 Minutes.
Inscription:
Sgt Co G 3 Infantry World War I

Jesse E Hudgens
Birth:
Dec. 5, 1862
Cheatham County,
Tennessee
Death:
Aug. 17, 1952
Ashland City
Cheatham County,
Tennessee
Burial:
Hudgens Cemetery
Cheatham County,
Tennessee

He gave fifty years of ministry and service to the Free Will Baptist denomination.

Rev George Virgil Johnson, Jr
Birth
31 Jan 1937
Death
31 Mar 2018
Troy,
Oakland County, Michigan
Burial
Plainview Cemetery
White County, Tennessee

Rev. George Johnson of Warren, Michigan, passed away in Troy Beaumont Hospital after a short battle with cancer.

George was born to George V. Johnson, Sr. and Jessie 'Lena' Brown Johnson.

He married Mary Glenn on February 15, 1957.

Ordained in 1965, he served as pastor of Free Will Baptist churches in both Tennessee and Michigan for over 50 years. At the time of his death, he was faithfully pastoring re at North Warren FWB Church in Warren, where he had served for 47 years.

Richard M Johnson
Birth:
1851
Death:
1913
Burial:
Alder-Livesay Cemetery,
Kyles Ford,
Hancock County, Tennessee

Rev G. G. Joyner
Birth:
Jan. 17, 1880
Death:
Sep. 4, 1964
Burial:
Parsons Cemetery
Parsons
Decatur County
Tennessee

Ordained Free Will Baptist minister in Tenn.

Matthias Judd
Birth:
May 30, 1844
Putnam County
Tennessee
Death:
Feb. 2, 1925
Cookeville
Putnam County
Tennessee
Burial:
Judd Church Cemetery
Cookeville
Putnam County
Tennessee

Rev. Matthias Judd was the son of Rev. Nathaniel Judd, whose property the cemetery was on. He was affilated with the Free Will Baptist, and his name appears in a list of ordained ministers, in 1879 Conference Minutes. He served in 1st Tennessee Mounted Infantry Regiment USA Union Roster during the Civil War. Enlisted on Aug 20,

1864 and Mustered on Jan 7, 1865 in Company I as a Corporal. Promoted from Private Jan 7, 1865 1st Matthias married Mary Bullington 14 Jan 1864 in Cookeville, Putnam Co, TN. Mary was the daughter of George Washington Bullington and Malinda Grinder. Mary was born 7 April 1847 in Putnam Co, TN and died 26 Mar 1902 in Cookeville, Putnam Co, TN.

Matthias Judd and Mary Bullington had a son, Nathan Alpheus Judd born 11 May 1865 in Cookeville, TN and died 11 April 1940 in Lubbock Texas.

2nd Matthias married Mary Ellen Smith 12 Apr 1903 in Cookeville, Putnam Co, TN. Mary Ellen was born 27 Nov 1870 in Cumberland Co, Kentucky, and died 6 April 1937 in Putnam Co, TN.

Rev Nathaniel Jackson Judd, Sr
Birth:
Sep. 5, 1807
Adair County, Kentucky
Death:
Mar. 21, 1885
Cookeville
Putnam County,
Tennessee
Burial:
Judd Church Cemetery
Cookeville
Putnam County,
Tennessee

He was a minister/pastor in the Old Stone Association of Christian Baptist Church, org. 1835, which later united with the Free Will Baptist in Tenn. Rev. Nathaniel Judd is listed in the names of FWB ordained ministers in Minutes of Old Stone Ass'n, when convened at Laurel Creek church, Cumberland Co. TN, Fri. Oct. 3, 1879. There was also a Rev. M. Judd, in the same listing.

His grandfather was Rowland Judd {1720-1801} DAR Library # A063428

His parents were John Judd {1761-1765-1 Oct 1823 Adair Co KY} DAR Library # A208840 and Polly {b.1775-d.Sept 1839 Adair Ky}

A son of Rowland Judd was Robert Judd 1766-1847} he was married to Rachel Greer {b.1770} who was a daugther of Benjamin Greer and Nancy Wilkerson who was a daugther of Sarah Boone sister to the Frontiersman Daniel Boone.

Paul Jackson Ketteman
Birth:
Jul. 24, 1924
Illinois
Death:
May 21, 1987
Nashville,
Davidson County, Tennessee
Burial:
Harpeth Hills Memory Gardens,
Nashville, Davidson County,
Tennessee

Paul J. Ketteman, was on the college's first graduating class in 1942. In May 1945, Paul graduated from the new school's two year program after working hard to pay for his education. He immediately enrolled in Columbia Bible College, Columbia, S. C. To finish his degree in 1947. Paul pastored first at Mt. Elon FWB Church, then at Edgemont FWB Church in Durham, North Carolina, then back to Mt. Elon (this time full-time), and later at First FWB Church, Columbus,

Mississippi. He served four years as clerk of the National Association of Free Will Baptists and nine years on the Bible College Board Of Trustees. He worked for the college 25 years in fundraising and public relations. His wife, Mrs. Helen Ketteman, taught business 20 years at the college.

Paul was a native of Illinois and was raised in a minister's home. His life was totally dedicated to his Lord and the college that he represented. He began the annual Christmas fund drive that was given his name after his death. He understood better than most how costly it is to provide Christian education. The idea of challenging churches and individuals to operate the college for a day originated with the Paul J. Ketteman, long time public relations director at FWBBC.

Dewey R Kirk
Birth:
Jan. 18, 1937
Death:
Jun. 25, 1982
Burial:

Island Ford Cemetery,
Lake City,
Anderson County, Tennessee

Jesse Laws
Birth:
1889
Death:
1931
Burial:
Laws-Green Cemetery,
Cocke County,
Tennessee

William Wallace Lee
Birth:
Nov. 26, 1857
Hawkins County, Tennessee
Death:
Aug. 28, 1944
Sullivan County, Tennessee
Burial:
Collins - Gravelly Rd
Sullivan County, Tennessee

His name is in early FWB records. Pastored at the Morning Star Freewill Baptist Church Hawkins County, TN

Roy Lee Lester, Jr
Birth
23 Apr 1951
Pineville, Wyoming County, West Virginia
Death
8 May 2018
Kingsport, Sullivan County, Tennessee

Burial
East Lawn Memorial Park Cemetery
Kingsport, Sullivan County, Tennessee

Roy Lee Lester, Jr., 67, Kingsport, TN, went home at Wellmont Holston Valley Medical Center, after a lingering illness.

He was born to Roy Lee Lester, Sr. and Venis Lucille Bledsoe Lester in Pineville, WV.

He asked Jesus to be his Lord and Savior in 1969, the same year he graduated from Oceana High School, Oceana, WV. After high school, he attended West Virginia University. While there, he felt the call of the Lord ...

He transferred to Free Will Baptist Bible College in Nashville, TN. He got married before he completed his degree. But, he always had a thirst for knowledge! He continued his education through Bluefield College, Bluefield, WV, earning a degree of Bachelor of Science. Next, he earned both a Master of Religious Education and a Doctor of Religious Education from Bethany Theological Seminary, Dothan, Alabama. Then, he earned both a Master of Letter and a Doctor of Letters from Cambridge Institute of Theology, Bristol, VA.

Roy Lee has been in the ministry since 1970, pastoring full time in churches in Virginia, West Virginia, Michigan and Tennessee. In his journey, he volunteered his time in rescue squads, nursing homes, assisted living facilities, as well as serving as Chaplain in the TN National Guard. Besides pastoring, he taught in Christian schools and seminaries.

Rev James Wilson Lucas

BIRTH
3 Mar 1850
North Carolina

DEATH
23 Jun 1916 (aged 66)
Knoxville, Knox County, Tennessee

BURIAL
Swingle Cemetery
Unicoi, Unicoi County, Tennessee

Rev. James Wilson Lucas, son of Alfred and Penelope (Giles) Lucas, was born near Averysboro, N.C.. He was married to Miss Julia Creech, July 21, 1875, and they had four daughters. He consecrated his life to God in September 1863; he received license to preach in 1868 and was ordained in 1872. He was a graduate of Wake Forest College. He was active in the ministry within the Cape Fear Free Will Baptist Conference in North Carolina until 1881, when he relocated to East Tennessee as pastor of the Woolsey College Church in Greene County, in the Union Association of Free Will Baptists. He continued to be active in that association until his death, except for a few years when he was in the Unicoi Free Will Baptist Association, which he helped establish. His most lengthy pastorates were of the Midway and Unicoi churches. He was also engaged in teaching and was founder and principal of high schools in Parrottsville, Midway, and Unicoi, all in Tennessee. He participated in the triennial General Conference of Free Baptists (of the North) in 1901, 1904, and 1907 and enlisted that body's aid in buying property in Unicoi and establishing the Free Will Baptist school there. It opened in 1903 and continued under his leadership, with limited success, until about 1908; in 1916 the General Conference abandoned the project and sold the property to Unicoi County for a public school. Lucas died in that same year and the following obituary appears in the minutes of the Union Association of Free Will Baptists for 1918:

IN MEMORIAM:

Resolved: That we bow in humble submission to the will of the Master in taking from our midst our beloved leader and wise counsellor, Rev. J.W. Lucas, who departed this life, June 23rd, at Lincoln Memorial Hospital in Knoxville. His native state was North Carolina, where he spent his early boyhood days. At the age of 13 he professed faith in Christ, and ever since took an active interest in church work and was always a leader in any duties pertaining to the church. He was a devoted Christian and suffered many unmerited persecutions which he took good naturedly, and yet amidst all this, his wonderful brain power made him a great factor in every community in which he resided.

He graduated Wake Forest College, N.C., and was a life-long student whose brain capacity measured up to the standard of the great men of our Nation.

He came to Woolsey College in 1881, and immediately affiliated himself with the work of educating and organizing the churches of the Mountain Free Baptists. He established schools at Parrottsville, Midway and Unicoi, for the express purpose of educating our poor Free Baptist children and ministers under adverse and trying circumstances; he struggled hard to maintain them, but by no fault of his own he failed. His example before his people and his followers will be missed, but he has gone to receive the reward of the final faithful where there is no sorrow, no pain, no persecutions, no death. --T.H. Woolsey, J.L. Cagle, Wm. Stroup, Committee.

James Willard McCarroll
Birth:
Aug. 12, 1935
Death:
Jan. 5, 2009
Joelton,
Davidson County,
Tennessee
Burial:
Joelton Hills Memory Gardens,
Joelton,

Davidson County, Tennessee

He was a Minister of the Gospel for over 45 years and pastored four churches; Harper Road Free Will Baptist Church, Mount Zion Free Will Baptist Church, First Free Will Baptist Church of McEwen and was currently serving the Olivet Free Will Baptist Church in Clarksville, all in Tennessee.

Elmer Daniel McCowan
BIRTH
29 Jan 1937
Overton County, Tennessee, USA
DEATH
25 Apr 2015 (aged 78)
Cookeville, Putnam County, Tennessee, USA
BURIAL
Harris Chapel Cemetery
Livingston,

Overton County, Tennessee

Elmer D. McCowan, Age 78. He was Born in Dry Hollow Community, to the Late; Johnnie and Willie [Pippin] McCowan-He was a Minister of Free Will Baptist Church for Forty-Three.

Rev George Washington McCowan
BIRTH
31 Mar 1868
Kingston, Roane County, Tennessee, USA
DEATH
31 Mar 1947 (aged 79)
Overton County, Tennessee, USA
BURIAL
Moses Wilson Cemetery
Overton County, Tennessee

The Free Will Baptist Denomination as we know it today has experienced considerable growth in the last 50 years. Much of it is due to the foundation laid by many of our Pioneer preachers the former years. One of them is the late Rev. George Washington McCowan.

He was called the Pioneer Preacher and preached for the Free Will Baptists for 44 years. Bro. Oliver stated that he lived with his grandfather when he was 12 years old and learned many things from him, even as a boy. Rev. George W. Pastor Tyler Point FWB Church for 17 years. Other pastorates in Banner Springs in Morgan County, Columbia Hill and Union B Church, plus he organized Union Grove Church, and was busy preaching revivals. One year he reported 279 sermons preached, witnessed over 70 conversions and baptized 65. He was the father of three girls and five boys. He was a great singer and his favorite songs were Wayfaring Pilgrim, How Firm A Foundation and on Jordan's Stormy Banks I Stand.

He was a member of the Eastern Division of the stone Association. In 1940 Bro. Charles Miller (Pioneer Deacon in Hazel Park Church in Mich.) sent for Bro. George W. to come to Michigan for revival. Bro. McCowan usually did his travelling by horseback and did not have the money to go to Michigan. Bro. Miller him $100.00 to make the trip, and Mr. Gilbert Looper drove him to Detroit and the A-model

Ford and the church experienced a good meeting with this 'Pioneer Preacher!' Rev. George W. McCowan has five (5) grandsons that are faithful F.W.B. preachers. They are, Elmer McCowan, Oliver McCowan, Daley McCowan, Tommy Vaughn and Talmadge Phillips.

Henry Melvin
Birth:
Jul. 8, 1905
Death:
Jun., 1971
Nashville, Davidson County, Tennessee
Burial:
Spring Hill Cemetery, Nashville, Davidson County, Tennessee

Brother Melvin was saved in a Methodist revival in Kynesville, Florida at the age of 17 and later surrendered to God's call to the ministry. He was ordained on October 3, 1925 in that city. In his early ministry. He pastored in Florida and Georgia. Prior to the formation of the National Association in 1935 brother Melvin attended the General Conference for the first time in 1927. This conference dates back to 1920. Melvin preached the opening sermon the very next year in 1928. He was a frequent program personality thereafter, including messages in 1928 and 1932. He was a leader in Christian Education illustrated by his service on the annual education committee in 1929 and in 1931.

In 1929 he was elected General Secretary Of Young People Word for the General Conference. Many acknowledge that the most significant contribution to his denomination was his ministry to the youth--first with the League Board and later the Church Training Service Board. Altogether, he served 39 years with The League and CTS board. He was known for his energetic and visionary leadership which kept the youth board moving ahead for Christ. He showed his interest in mission's early serving on the annual missions committee of the convention in 1927 and again in 1932. The 1932 minutes show that his sermon was on "The Church" and he strongly emphasized the church's mission in bringing the world to Christ. In 1935, he was very instrumental in producing an atmosphere of optimism in the merger of the Western and Eastern conferences. Following the report of the committee, brother Melvin suggested that all stand and sing, *Blessed Be The Tie That Binds,* as a token of the reality of the coming tie. In the mid-30's brother Melvin pastored the Edgemont Free Will Baptist Church in Durham, North Carolina. It was here that a close relationship between he and Thomas and Mabel Willey came into existence and he introduced them to the Free Will Baptist Missions program where they later served under their auspices. At the Seventh Annual Session of the national association in Nashville, Tennessee in 1943, the Board Of Foreign Missions commended him for his involvement in the missions program by sponsoring a trip for him to Cuba in February, 1943, during which time he assisted Rev. and Mrs. Willey in the organization of the Cuban national convention..

In 1946 he was elected to the Free Will Baptists Bible College Board of Trustees. He was the college business manager the following year. Because of his strong musical talents he was selected to the 1964 music committee for the new Free Will Baptist hymn book. He was a well-respected pastor with at least

26 sons in the ministry during those pastorates.

His son, Dr. Billy Melvin, became the Executive-Secretary of the National Association of Free Will Baptists and later the Director of the National Association Of Evangelicals.

Trymon Messer
Birth:
Nov. 13, 1932
Pontotoc,
Mississippi
Death:
Jan. 10, 2015
Nashville
Davidson County,
Tennessee
Burial:
Middle Tennessee State Veterans
Cemetery
Nashville
Davidson County,
Tennessee

The former U.S. Marine who brought home four medals from Korea began practicing what drill instructors taught him on Paris Island—leadership.

As Lay pastor for 11 years in Salina, Kansas, the congregation mushroomed to a record attendance of 859, completed three building programs, and helped start five Kansas churches. He chaired the Kansas Mission Board and was elected to Hillsdale FWB College's Board of Trustees. Wherever he went, people stepped up to follow his leadership. The National Association elected him to the Home Missions Board in 1973.

Twice named Layman of the Year—in 1964 by Hillsdale FWB College and in 1969 by Master's Men—Messer was sought by pastors nationwide to lead church-growth conferences.

When Trymon was 45 years old, the Home Missions Department named him associate director (1978), where his practical biblical knowledge and sense of humor made him one of the agency's top spokesmen. He was named general director in 1995 and completed 22 years with the department.

Trymon Messer lived by a simple philosophy: "I believe that if a man will claim God's promise, practice God's presence, and demonstrate God's power, he cannot fail."

LaVerne Dale Miley
Birth:
Sep. 9, 1928
Kirksville,
Adair County, Missouri
Death:
Mar. 15, 2005
Nashville,
Davidson County, Tennessee
Burial:
Woodlawn Memorial Park,
Nashville,
Davidson County, Tennessee

A Free Will Baptist minister, medical doctor, missionary, and college professor. He opened the medical work in the Ivory Coast, Africa, where he served as a medical missionary for 19 years. For many years he was a professor at the Free Will Baptist Bible College in Nashville, Tennessee and served as a medical consultant for Free Will Baptist International Missions. He also worked with the Navajo Indians in the western United States and served in the Men of Valor Prison Ministry and was a longtime member of Cofer's Chapel Free Will Baptist Church in Nashville, Tennessee.

William H Morelock
Birth:
1875
Death:
1956
Burial:
Beech Creek Missionary Baptist Church Cemetery, Rogersville, Hawkins County, Tennessee

Rev Joseph Wesley Moyers
Birth:
May 31, 1854
Death:
Oct. 13, 1934
Burial:
Cox Cemetery
Claiborne County
Tennessee

Rev. Joseph A. Moyers, was an ordained Free Will Baptist minister in the Stone Association, as shown in its Annual Minutes, Oct. 3, 1879, when meeting with the Laurel Creek church, Cumberland Co. TN: "...On motion, and in pursuance of Section 9 of the Declaration of Rights, there were appointed as Presbyters, Elders T. J. Clouse, John Brewster, Joseph A. Moyers, G. L. Moyers and John Stowers for the next associational year. On motion, the ministers were appointed to attend the several churches as pastors..." [Then it gives names of several churches in the group.] Evidently, Rev. Moyers was a leader and esteemed minister who was given responsibilities they thought he would faithfully carry out. Nothing at this time is known regarding the year he was ordained. Husband of Elizabeth Jane Eastridge Moyers. Son of Abraham Wheeler Jefferson & Anna Goin Moyers

Howard T. Munsey
Birth:
Jun. 27, 1926
Death:
Aug. 14, 2009
Burial:
Jefferson Memorial Gardens Cemetery, Jefferson City, Jefferson County, Tennessee

He was the founding pastor of Peace Free Will Baptist Church in Morristown, delivered his first sermon in 1953 at Greenville First Free Will Baptist Church. He joined the U.S. Navy in 1942 and served during World War II and the Korean War, achieving the rank of petty officer first class. Rev. Munsey worked for Magnavox, built homes, and later part-owner of Hearthstone Log Homes in Dandridge during the 1970s and 1980s. During his lifetime, he organized two and pastored seven other Free Will Baptist churches. He had an effective revival and pulpit-supply ministry. Rev. Munsey served as the president, until his death, of Berea Ministries

Inc., a mission organization he created in the 1950s to support the ministry of national pastors in Mexico. It was first chartered as the mission arm of a radio ministry called "Cross Beams Missions."

James Harrison Oliver
Birth:
Apr. 6, 1882
Cadiz, Kentucky
Death:
Jun. 8, 1939
Burial:
Hays/Hayes Cemetery
Stewart County,Tennessee

Parents: William Harrison Oliver (1847 - 1929)- Susan Litchfield Oliver (1849 - 1931)
Spouse: Frances L Hembree Oliver (1884 - 1960)
Children: William Henry Oliver (1903 - 1991), James Herschel Oliver (1910 - 2007), Myrtle Oliver Stanley (1914 - 2005), Pearl Oliver Miller (1917 - 2007).

James Alan Munsey
Birth:
Aug. 10, 1950
Death:
Feb. 3, 2001
Texas
Burial:
Union Cemetery, Newport,
Cocke County, Tennessee

Munsey built the Free Will Baptist Church in Weslaco, Texas, while he worked with Free Will Baptist churches in Mexico. He was very instrumental in building many churches in Mexico and organizing numerous ones. He also was instrumental in building a Free Will Baptist Institute for the training of Mexican pastors. He was the son of Howard Munsey.

William Henry Oliver
Birth:
Nov. 4, 1903
Indian Mound
Stewart County, Tennessee
Death:
May 15, 1991
Nashville
Davidson County, Tennessee
Burial:
Forest Lawn Memorial Gardens
Goodlettsville
Davidson County, Tennessee

Rev. Dr. William Henry Oliver, a Free Will Baptist minister for 68 years, in Nashville. Hundreds attended his funeral May 18 at East High School where he served 18 years as principal (1939-1957). Rev. Oliver once said in an interview that he had three goals in mind when he started college---to become a preacher, a teacher and a writer. He eventually accomplished all three. "I felt the Lord wanted me to be a preacher. I had to be a teacher, and I wanted to be a writer," he said. Mr. Oliver began teaching in Nashville city schools in 1930 at Hume Fogg HS. He taught algebra and English and coached the school's boxing and baseball teams, leading the baseball players to a city championship. He received his bachelor's degree from Vanderbilt University in 1926, and later received master's degrees in arts and education at George Peabody College. In 1957, the Nashville Board of education elected Mr. Oliver as city school superintendent. He retired in 1963 after the city and county government merged. He taught at Belmont College for the next seven years and then took a similar position at Free Will Baptist Bible College (1970-1977).He was ordained a minister in 1924 and later founded and became the first pastor of the East Nashville Free Will Baptist Church. He wrote literature and poetry including one well received poem titled At Twilight. In 1987 he was awarded an honorary Doctor of Literature Letters from Cumberland University. He was a member of the Kappa Alpha fraternity, Civitan, the Red Cross board, past president of the East Nashville YMCA and a past member of the Nashville Chamber of Commerce.

Rev Tim Anthony Osborn
Birth:
Jan. 22, 1964
Russellville
Franklin County, Alabama
Death:
May 17, 2014
Memphis
Shelby County, Tennessee
Burial:
Fayette County Memorial Park
Oakland
Fayette County, Tennessee

He received his education in the Alabama Public School System and was a graduate of the Baptist Bible College in Nashville, Tennessee. He was married *December 21, 1985 to the former* Robyn Barnes of Farmington, Missouri, who currently serves as a teacher at the Macon Road Baptist Church School. Pastor Osborn had been a minister for over 25 years and had formerly served pastorates in North Carolina and was involved in church missions in the Memphis area before serving in Fayette County. Anyone that knew Tim knew without question that his God and his family were his passions and his church family was an important part of his life. At the time of his death, Pastor Osborn served as the chaplain for the Macon Fire Department in Macon, Tennessee. The officiating ministers were David Crowe, Richard Atwood and Michael Gillock. Graveside Services followed in the Fayette County Memorial Park Cemetery on Highway 64 with remarks given by Gwyn Pugh.

Hardy C Pace
Birth:
May 30, 1846
Death:
Oct. 16, 1928
Burial:
Taylor Cemetery
Stewart County, Tennessee

He served as a Free Will Baptist minister in the Ashland Quarterly Meeting in the late 1800s. He was married to D Attie Wallace Pace (1847 - 1929)

Preacher Pate loved sports and was a dedicated supporter of Bearden High School and the University of Tennessee, but more than sports, he loved God's work. He worked tirelessly raising funds for International Missions through his yearly walk-a-thons. He also was a Barber for over 50 years.
Funeral services was at Bridges Funeral Home with Rev. Jerry Gibbs officiating.

Rev. Thurman McLain Pate, Sr
Birth:
February 13, 1920
Death:
January 16, 2019
Knoxville, Tennessee
Burial:
Greenwood Cemetery
Knoxville, Tennessee

Thurman pastored for over 70 years in several Free Will Baptist Churches, the last 40 years serving at Faith Free Will Baptist Church.

Rev Jesse Benton Parsons
Birth
3 Nov 1901
Unionville, Bedford County, Tennessee, Usa

Death
3 Mar 1990 (Aged 88)
Pleasant View, Cheatham County, Tennessee, Usa

Burial
Good Springs Free Will Baptist
Church Cemetery
Pleasant View, Cheatham
County, Tennessee, Usa

Rev Billy Gene Outland
Birth:
Mar. 25, 1935
Kenly
Johnston County
North Carolina
Death:
Mar. 9, 2015
Nashville
Davidson County
Tennessee
Burial:

Harpeth Hills Memory Gardens
Nashville
Davidson County
Tennessee

Long-time Free Will Baptist pastor and denominational leader passed from this life at Saint Thomas Hospital in Nashville after years of declining health. His wife Peggy preceded him in death. He is survived by their daughter Angela (Mark) Trotter and a granddaughter Audrey Jordan (Blake). The Outland's last pastorate was the Hazel Dell Free Will Baptist Church in Sesser, Illinois. They moved back to Tennessee after retirement a few years ago. Before moving to Illinois, they served the Cofer's Chapel Free Will Baptist Church in Nashville.

Rev Talmage Phillips
BIRTH
25 Jan 1930
Overton County,
Tennessee, USA

DEATH
20 Jan 2004 (aged 73)
Monterey,
Putnam County,
Tennessee, USA
BURIAL
F A Norrod Memorial Cemetery
Hanging Limb,
Overton County,
Tennessee, USA

Rev. Phillips died at Standing Stone Care and Rehab Center in Monterey. He had been a minister since he was 18 years-old and served several area Freewill Baptist churches. He founded the 25th Street Freewill Baptist Church in Anderson, IN, which was the first Freewill Baptist Church in that state.

He sang with the Talmage Phillips Singers for more than 50 years, was active in the Crawford Community, and was one of the founders of Hanging Limb Community Center.

Rev. Phillips was a former road superintendent with Overton County Highway Department and was a retired staff member of Horner Funeral Home.

He was the son of the late Perry Phillips and Ruby (Vaughn) Phillips Harville.

Jerry Franklin Presley
Birth:
Jan. 16, 1932
Death:
Sep. 28, 1993
Tennessee
Burial:
Sweetwater Valley Memorial Park,
Sweetwater,
Monroe County, Tennessee

He was a Free Will Baptist minister and pastor for 26 years in Tennessee and Illinois until poor health forced him to resign from full-time pastoral service. He held numerous denominational positions, including Promotional-Secretary for the Tennessee Union Association, Youth camp Director, and 10 years as clerk of the Union Ministerial Association. He taught school in four Tennessee counties. He served in Korea with the U.S. Army.

Fannie Lee Binkley Polston
Birth: 1881
Death:
Apr. 24, 1964
Nashville
Davidson County
Tennessee
Burial:
Spring Hill Cemetery
Nashville
Davidson County,Tennessee
Plot: Sect G

Daughter of Henry J. and Rhoda (Sanders) Binkley. Married Frederick Polston in 1903. One daughter, Irene, born to this union Employed as a pantry maid in a hotel before marrying Fred.

Mrs. Polston 64 Dies at 82

Mrs. Fannie Lee Polston, 82, of 513 Woodland St., one of the founders of Nashville Free Will Bible College, died yesterday morning in Miller's Hospital after a heart attack.

Services will be at 10 a.m. Sunday at East Nashville Free Will Baptist Church. The Rev. J. L. Welch, the Rev. Henry Melvin and Dr. L. C. Johnson will officiate. Burial will be in Spring Hill Cemetery.

The body is at Cosmopolitan Funeral Home.

A NATIVE of Ashland City, she was a daughter of Henry J. and Rhoda Sanders Binkley. She attended Cheatham County public schools and was married in 1902 to Fred Polston. He died in 1933.

Mrs. Polston organized the West Nashville Free Will Baptist Church in 1924 and was a charter member. She was the current president of the Nashville Women's Christian Temperance Union and had been a member of the board of Eureka College in Ayden, N.C.

Mrs. Polston was one of the founders of the Nashville Free Will Baptist Bible College in 1942 and continued to take an active part in the college up to the time of her death.

Mrs. Polston also was instrumental in the founding of Free Will Baptist Children's Home in Greenville, Tenn.

Survivors are a daughter, Mrs. Irene Coville, Morehead City, N.C.; a sister, Mrs. T. W. Maxey, Ashland City; three grandchildren, Mrs. Eve Griffin, Nashville, Mrs. Flaines Waider, Morehead City and William Coville, Akron, Ohio, and four great-grandchildren.

Cleo Pursell
Birth:
Feb. 16, 1918
Fort Worth,
Tarrant County,
Texas
Death:
Dec. 17, 2009
Nashville,
Davidson County
, Tennessee
Burial:
Woodlawn Memorial Park and
Mausoleum, Nashville,
Davidson County, Tennessee

Twenty-one year old Cleo (Dalton) Pursell, ordained by the West Fork District Association in 1939.

She became the first full-time Executive Sec. of the Women's National Auxiliary Convention and led the organization for 22 years (1963-1985). The headquarters of this woman's organization is located in Nashville, Tennessee and is part of the National Association of Free Will Baptists. The ministry flourished under her capable leadership and eventually she led the membership to an all-time high. She was a prolific writer of books and pamphlets as well as writing a regular feature for *Contact* Magazine called "Words for Women". She will be remembered for her far-reaching vision and constant leadership. She was 91 at her passing. She was an ordained minister and outlived her minister husband, Rev. Paul Purcell, who is buried in Oklahoma.

Rev. Russell Owen Raulston
Birth
22 Dec 1856
Marion County, Tennessee

Death
7 Jul 1938 (Aged 81)
Chattanooga,
Hamilton County,
Tennessee

Burial
Chattanooga Memorial Park
Chattanooga,
Hamilton County,
Tennessee

Roger C Reeds
Birth:
Sep. 16, 1928
Saint Louis,
St. Louis City, Missouri
Death:
May 2, 2007
Joelton,
Davidson County, Tennessee
Burial:
Joelton Hills Memory Gardens,
Joelton,
Davidson County, Tennessee

A Free Will Baptist pastor, author, and denominational leader. Converted in November 9, 1947 and called to preach the next year. He pastored churches in Missouri, North Carolina, and Tennessee. He was the founding Director of Randall House Publications, in Nashville, Tennessee, where he served 31 years, and was on the committee of founders of Donelson Christian Academy. He held degrees from Free Will Baptist Bible College, Middle Tennessee State University and Luther Rice Seminary.

Norman Howard Richards
Birth:
Sep. 30, 1938
White County, Arkansas
Death:
Aug. 22, 2013
Nashville
Davidson County, Tennessee
Burial:
Mount Olivet Cemetery
Nashville
Davidson County, Tennessee

Norman age 74, of Nashville, passed away at the Vanderbilt Medical Center. He faithfully loved and served the Lord as a Missionary in Africa and as a Minister, presently with The Donelson Fellowship Church. He was preceded in death by his parents; 2 brothers and 1 sister. Rev. Richards is survived by his loving wife of 50 years, Bessie Richards; sons, Gene Richards (Patti), and Randal Richards (Patty); 4 grandchildren, Wesley, Julia, Olivia, and David; 2 brothers,

Wayne Richards (Patsy) and Claude Presnell (Juanita); and 3 sisters, Mildred Sowell, Juanita Dickson (Ray), and Madie Walker (Don). Funeral services were conducted at the church with the Rev. Robert Morgan officiating. A private family graveside service was conducted in the Mount Olivet Cemetery.

Charles Raymond Riggs
Birth:
Oct. 15, 1915
Randolph County, Arkansas
Death:
Apr. 13, 2009
Burial:
Crest Lawn Cemetery,
Cookeville,
Putnam County, Tennessee

In November of 1934, he was married to Velma Staten and she passed away two months later. He then was united in marriage to Winona Mae Gates on October 25, 1936. She preceded him in death in March 1999.

Then he married Burnice Davis on July 22, 1999, in Cookeville, Tennessee. Brother Riggs was in his early ministry a schoolteacher, and as a minister known for his singing. He became an outstanding pastor and minister in the Detroit area. Under his leadership as the first Director Of Foreign Missions for the National Association of Free Will Baptist the organization grew. He is remembered as an early statesman for the denomination and has left a legacy of having many sons and grandchildren as ministers within the denomination.

Paul Robinson
Bieth:
June 20, 1925
Tennessee
Death:
August 19, 2018.
Burial:
Unknown

Paul Robinson, pioneer missionary to Uruguay, was transported from his home in Smithville, Tennessee, to Vanderbilt Veterans Hospital in Nashville, Tennessee, following a fall on Saturday, the 93-year-old died of cardiac arrest.

Appointed as missionaries to Uruguay in 1960, Paul and his wife Amy departed for language school in Costa Rica in August 1961. They teamed with Bill and Glenda Fulcher to plant churches along the border with Brazil. Working in rural areas outside the border-town of Rivera, the Robinsons also developed a camp for church members. A natural evangelist, Paul's love for people translated into a desire to see them know His Savior. Paul, who never considered himself anything other than a layman, believed his status encouraged Uruguayan laymen to serve and be witnesses. The Robinsons retired from missionary service in 1992, after 32 years of service with IM. They continued ministering to Hispanics after they settled in Smithville.

Born and raised in Tennessee, Paul served in the Navy from 1943-1946, participating in five invasions in that short span.

Although 25 years old when he came to Christ, his conversion served to instill a burden for Latin America in his heart. Living in the Detroit area, he attended Highland Park Free Will Baptist Church (now Central Oaks Community Church) to hear Cuban pastor Benito Rodriguez preach. Benito, a product of Pop and Mom Willey's ministry in Cuba, led this future missionary to Christ. Paul served Highland Park as a layman, met and married Amy (Lucaciu), studied at Detroit Bible Institute, and attended Berlitz School of Languages at night. While serving at Hyde Park, Paul constantly interacted with missionaries. Finally, he surrendered to overseas service and the family of three moved to Nashville, Tennessee, to attend Free Will Baptist Bible College (now Welch College) for one year before heading to language school..

Carol A. Waring Robirds
Birth:
Mar. 8, 1938
California

Death:
Mar. 30, 2010
Brentwood,
Davidson County,
Tennessee
Burial:
Woodlawn Memorial Park and
Mausoleum,Nashville,
Davidson County,Tennessee

Carol and her husband, Don, served as FWB missionaries in Brazil from 1964 to 1971, when Don was asked to join the office staff in Nashville as Dir. of Communications. Carol served as his assistant for several years.

Willie B Rodgers
Birth:
Jun. 14, 1918
Putnam County, Tennessee
Death:
Feb. 7, 2005
Cookeville
Putnam County, Tennessee
Burial:
Rodgers Cemetery
Baxter
Putnam County, Tennessee

Rev. Willie B. Rodgers passed away at his home. He was 86 years of age, and a native of Putnam Co. TN. Bro. Rodgers had a very fruitful ministry in South and North Carolina, and Tennessee. Most of his ministery was in Tenn. Churches he pastored: Antioch; Lily's Chapel; Duncan's Chapel; Manchester First; Trinity (Nashville); Taylor's Providence; Post Oak Shade; Algood First; United Hensley's Chapel; Taylor's Seminary; Cedar Hill; and Community Church.Rev. Jack Taylor conducted his service. He commented that he had many times sought good counsel from Bro. Rodgers. He was a devoted Bible student. He lived what he preached and was a great influence to many people. He married Velma Ramsey Rodgers.

Inscription:
Married April 28, 1950;
PFC US Army WWII

Rev John Russell
Birth:
Jan. 15, 1814
Death:
Jan. 26, 1905
Tennessee
Burial:
Sims Cemetery
Sevier County
Tennessee

His name and dates are listed in Free Baptist Cyclopedia, for TN, with other ministers serving in NE TN in the 1887 roster.

Melvin R Sanford
Birth:
Jan. 31, 1920
Death:
Oct. 17, 1993
Burial:
Fairview Free Will Baptist Church Cemetery
Anderson County, Tennessee

He ministered for over 54 years and started several churches in West Virginia pastoring numerous churches there. He also pastored churches in Ohio and Florida. He was known for his revivals some of which went as much as six weeks or more. He saw a great number of converts during his ministry. He was married to Helen L Sanford (1925 - 1998)
Inscription:
Married June 23, 1943

Ernest Sawyer
Birth:
Unknown
Death:
Aug. 2, 2012
Del Rio, Cocke County, Tennessee
Burial:
Fugate Free Will Baptist Church Cemetery,
Del Rio, Cocke County, Tennessee

He pastored the Fugate Free Will Baptist church near Del Rio for 29 years.

Billie J Lay Sexton
Birth:
Feb. 13, 1934
Coxton, Kentucky
Death:
Dec. 20, 2015
Burial:
Happy Valley Memorial Park
Elizabethton
Carter County, Tennessee

She attended Virgie, Kentucky High School and Free Will Baptist Bible College, Nashville, Tennessee. She married Don Sexton, the love of her life, on December 23, 1950. Billie was a stay-at-home mom until Don became a minister and she became a dedicated pastor's wife, including learning to play the piano. Don and Billie pastored the Roan Street Free Will Baptist Church in the early 1960s in Elizabethton. They started the First

Free Will Baptist Church in Chattanooga, Tennessee, and Billie started working as a dental assistant to supplement the family income, while still very actively serving as a pastor's wife.

In 1972, at the ages of 42 & 38, Don & Billie answered the Lord's call and went to Switzerland to language school to learn French so they could start a Free Will Baptist Church in France. They first served the church in Nantes, France, then started a church in St. Nazaire, France. In 1979, when Don's health began to fail due to Parkinson's disease, they returned to the United States. Don & Billie worked tirelessly all across the country to raise money in support of foreign missions, which led to the creation of the annual Don & Billie Sexton Walk-A-Thon.

A Celebration of Life Service was held at Tetrick Funeral & Cremation Services, Johnson City with Wesley Simons officiating.

Donald Ray Sexton
Birth:
July 9, 1930
Kentucky
Death:
1997
Tennessee
Burial:
Happy Valley Memorial Park
Elizabethton
Carter County, Tennessee
Plot: Mausoleum of Peace

Sexton was licensed of preach in 1950 and ordained in 1951. He was a native of Jenkins, Kentucky. He graduated from Free Will Baptist Bible College in 1960 and attended language school in Switzerland and France. He served as Tennessee's first state missionary in 1963 and moderated the Tennessee State Association between 1967-71. He pastored six churches, four in Tennessee and two in Kentucky.

He and his wife Billie were missionaries to France beginning in 1971 and served until 1979 when Don was diagnosed with Parkinson's disease. During his ministry in France, Sexton started the First Free Will Baptist Church in in Nantes. He was elected the Field Director in 1976. After he returned to the states, Sexton was asked by the Foreign Mission Board to promote foreign missions in the United States. For the next 13 years he traveled, informed and motivated Free Will Baptist about foreign missions.

He resigned in 1990 due to his health problems. From his efforts the Don and Billi Sexton walk-a-thon became one of the most successful efforts in the denomination raising nearly 1,000,000 for missionary support.

Robert Logan Shockey
Birth:
Sep. 16, 1927
Clay City,
Powell County, Kentucky
Death:
Mar. 7, 2008
Chapmansboro,
Cheatham County, Tennessee
Burial:
Bet
Ashland City,
Cheatham County, Tennessee

He was called to preach in 1955 and ordained to preach in 1956. His education consisted of Bible Diploma/Free Will Baptist Bible College in Nashville, Tennessee, in 1958. His pastorates included Raccoon Free Will Baptist Church in

Greenup, Kentucky. From 1954-55; Bethlehem Free Will Baptist Church in Ashland City, Tennessee. From 1955-1957; Donelson Free Will Baptist Church in Nashville, Tennessee. from 1957-1959; Second Free Will Baptist Church in Ashland, Kentucky, from 1959-68 and 1973-74; Dothan Free Will Baptist Church in Dothan, Alabama from 1971 to 1973; Heritage Temple Free Will Baptist Church in Ashland, Kentucky from 1978-1984; Portland Free Will Baptist Church in Portland, Tennessee. in 2004. Denominational positions included: Moderator: Kentucky State Association of Free Will Baptists from 1959-1966; Moderator: Blue Grass Conference/Kentucky; Pastor of the Year Kentucky 1964; President: Bethel Bible Institute Paintsville, Kentucky from 1982-1984. Home Missions Department from 1961-1978; Member: Home Missions Board (1961-1966); Promotional Secretary (1967-1971); General Director (1972-1978) (includes Director of Evangelism and Director of Military Chaplains); Free Will Baptist Bible College 1984-1995; Campus Pastor, Christian Service Director, Ministerial Fellowship Director, Director of Student Support. National Radio Speaker Radio & TV Commission, Victorious Faith Program. Evangelist 1954-2008; United States/Canada/Mexico/Virgin Islands. His publications included Let's Go Fishing (pamphlet); How to Call a Pastor (pamphlet); Five Smooth Stones (pamphlet); The Teacher (pamphlet); Bus Ministry (pamphlet); How to Go Soul winning (pamphlet). Tracts include Gods Simple Plan of Salvation; Tip; Now That You Are Saved; Keys to a New Life. Other accomplishments include: United States Navy, Psychiatric Nurse, Served two enlistments.

Rolla Darrell Smith
Birth:
Dec. 29, 1920
Norwood, Wright County, Missouri
Death:
Mar. 15, 2013
Nashville, Davidson County, Tennessee
Burial:
Hermitage Memorial Gardens
Old Hickory, Davidson County, Tennessee

He pastored at Hazel Creek Free Will Baptist (FWB) Church (MO), Fellowship FWB Church (Flat River, MO), Donelson FWB Church

(Nashville), First FWB Church (Savannah, GA) and Grant Avenue FWB Church (Springfield, MO). He was a man of ordinary means yet rich in what matters most...love for God, love for family and love for friends. He was the General Director at FWB International Missions Department from 1960-1962 and 1975-1986 and Missions Instructor at Welch College from 1987-1989. Honorary Pallbearers were missionaries and staff members from the FWB International Missions Department and members of the Harvesters Sunday School Class at Cross Timbers FWB Church. A life celebration service was held at Harpeth Hills Funeral Home with Dr. Paul Harrison officiating.

Sam Peyton Stewart
Birth:
Jan. 18, 1857
Death:
Jun. 3, 1910
Burial:
Stewart Cemetery, Cookeville,
Putnam County, Tennessee

Rev. S. P. Stewart died at his home in the Seventh district. The news writer extends his sympathy to the bereaved family and friends. He was a Free-will Baptist minister. History of Putnam Co. TN Cane Creek Free Will Baptist membership roll shows Rev. Sam Peyton Stewart was a member there when he died in 1910. Samuel P. Stewart was the son of Jesse Peyton Stewart and Arminty Dorman Ray.

Rev Joseph Winfield Stone
Birth:
Aug. 30, 1869
Death:
Jan. 12, 1949
Burial:
Judd Church Cemetery
Cookeville
Putnam County
Tennessee

The Rev. J. W. Stone, 79, of Bloomington Springs, died suddenly of a heart attack Wednesday afternoon, 4½ miles west of Lebanon, while en route home from Nashville.

Rev. J. H. Roberson and the Rev. Oliver Lane officiated. The Rev. Stone was one of the oldest Baptist ministers of the Stone Association as well as this part of the State. He had been very active in the work of the Association having served as Moderator on many occasions and held a record of attending 50 consecutive annual meetings of the Association. He served, as pastor, practically every rural church in the Stone Association. He was ordained as a minister in 1896. However, he told his relatives only that he had preached for two years

before he was ordained. Rev. J.W. Stone's name is in a list of ministers of the Old Stone Association, which later united with the Free Will Baptist.

Rev John William Stowers
Birth:
Feb. 22, 1849
Loudon County
Tennessee
Death:
Mar. 25, 1932
Fentress County
Tennessee
Burial:
Springs Chapel Cemetery
Banner Springs
Fentress County
Tennessee

Minister in the Old Stone Association of Free Will Baptist, shown in Minutes in their 1879

session, with Laurel Creek Church, Cumberland Co. Tenn. He was married three times. Following are the Spouses:
Catherine Burton (1863 -1920), Jensy Emeline Brown Stowers (1851 - 1910), Matilda May Atkinson Stowers (1878 -1916).

Virginia Dawn Sweeney, age 57 of Nashville, TN was born to Rev. Quincy Winston and Fannie Jewel Addington Sweeney. She served in France and had to return because of failing health. Afterwards she worked in the Crisis Center for Family Ministries in Greenville, Tennessee. Ms. Sweeney was a graduate of Free Will Baptist Bible College.

She was preceded in death by her parents and is survived by her brother, Winston Larry Sweeney.

Missionary
Virginia Dawn Sweeney
Birth:
October 3,, 1958
Stacy,
North Carolina
Death:
January 5, 2016
Nashville,
Tennessee
Burial:
Cremated

William Jackson 'Jack' Taylor
Birth:
Oct. 24, 1936
Richmond, Virginia
Death:
Aug, 29, 2018
Cookeville Regional
Medical Center.
Burial:
Crest Lawn Cemetery

Rev. William Jackson "Jack" Taylor, 81, of Cookeville, held at Cookeville Freewill Baptist Church. Pastor

Charles Cook and Pastor Randy Hill officiated. He was born to the late William Harry and Sudie Elizabeth Cox Taylor.

Rev. Taylor was a member of Cookeville Freewill Baptist Church. Before entering the ministry, he was an associate with Georgia Boot Company and Borden Electric.

After being called into ministry, he served a number of area Freewill Baptist Churches including Post Oak Shade, Bethel, Gentry, Stone Seminary, and Taylor Seminary. He was Pastor at Monterey FWB Church for over 22 years along with hosting the Waves of Faith Radio Program on WHUB. He retired from the ministry after pastoring Forrest Grove FWB Church in Knoxville for more than seven years.He was a long-time member and chairman of Family Ministries Board of Directors, serving as field representative for 23 years.

He and Rev. Willie B. Rodgers were founders of Cookeville Regional Medical Center Chaplains.

William Horace Teague
Birth:
Aug. 2, 1918
Death:
Nov. 1, 2000
Burial:
Union Cemetery,
Newport
Cocke County,
Tennessee

He was called to preach in 1943 and was ordained in 1947 by Tennessee's union Association. He began passing immediately at Johnson's Chapel Free Will Baptist Church. He was a Free Will Baptist minister for 53 years and pastored a church is in his home state of Tennessee and for five years a church in Michigan. He then returned to Newport, Tennessee where he continued his ministry. He served as the moderator of the Tennessee state Association. He was a dedicated man who slap was fully yielded to Christ and he sacrificed for the ministry and suffered in order to preach the gospel. He had two sons that likewise became ministers Rev. Harold Teague of Beckville, Texas and Jim Teague of Chuckey, Tennessee

Elbert Worth Tippett

Birth:
Dec. 19, 1940
Portsmouth,
Portsmouth City,
Virginia
Jan. 5, 2011
Nashville,
Davidson County,
Tennessee
Burial:
Harpeth Hills Memory Gardens,
Nashville,
Davidson County,
Tennessee

Bert Tippett was the long-time voice of Free Will Baptist Bible College as he headed the media office for numerous years. He was a great preacher, gentleman and a person of sterling character.

Ray Carroll Turnage

Birth:
May 8, 1931
Lenoir County
North Carolina
Death:
Jun. 14, 2017
Oklahoma
Burial:
Oak Grove Freewill Baptist Church
Cemetery
Tusculum
Greene County
Tennessee

Ray Carroll Turnage was born to Roy Edward and Helen Onita (Abbott) Turnage. Ray was a graduate of Free Will Baptist Bible College in Nashville, TN and went on the get his M.E. from Middle TN State University in Murfreesboro, TN. He worked as a Superintendent at Free Will Baptist Home for Children in Greeneville, TN and retired from Greene County Schools. On August 23, 1953, Ray married Lissie (Chaudoin) Turnage, and together they shared 63 years of love, life, family, and friends. Ray was a member of the Heritage Baptist Church in Johnson City, TN, the Ruritan Club, an FFA Honorary Chapter Farmer and was presented the 1965 Free Will Baptist Layman of the Year award.

Ray is survived by his wife, Lissie; daughters, Vicki Toombs of Edmond, OK and Renee Brogan of Loganville, GA; grandchildren;

Beau Toombs of Chicago, IL, Amy Brogan of Cincinnati, OH, and David Brogan of Kennesaw, GA; sister, Nellie Turnage of West Columbia, SC; and sons-in-law, Larry Toombs of Edmond, OK.

Note: He was cremated and his remains are buried in the plot with his son Daniel in the same cemetery.

Rev Wendell Trussell
Birth:
Unknown
Death:
Oct. 6, 2014
Nashville
Davidson County, Tennessee
Burial:
Blantons Chapel Cemetery
Manchester
Coffee County, Tennessee

He served as pastor of the Faith Free Will Baptist Church in Manchester, Tennessee, where he served as pastor for thirty-one years. He had pastored Loyal Chapel in Columbia, Tennessee, the New Salem FWB church in Colquitt, Georgia and the Pelham FWB church, Pelham, Tennessee.

Rev Greg Tyson
Birth:
Mar. 18, 1959
Saint Louis
St. Louis City, Missouri

Death:
Aug. 3, 2014
Indian Mound
Stewart County, Tennessee
Burial:
Dunbar Chapel Cemetery
Stewart County, Tennessee

Rev. Greg Tyson, age 55 of Indian Mound, TN, went to be with the Lord on Sunday, August 3, 2014 at his residence.

Funeral services were held at Dunbar Chapel Freewill Baptist Church with Rev. Maxie Milliken and Rev. James Black officiating. He was born March 18, 1959 in St. Louis, MO son of James Noel and Ocie Milliken Tyson. Mr. Tyson received a bachelor's degree from Welch's Bible College, minister for over 27 years at Dunbar Chapel Freewill Baptist Church, had ministered at Brandon's Chapel Freewill Baptist Church and was safety coordinator of Nashville Wire.

R. Eugene Waddell
Birth:
1935
Death:
Oct. 21, 2007
Burial:
Harpeth Hills
Memory Gardens, Nashville,,
Davidson County, Tennessee

He served with distinction churches in South Carolina, Virginia, and North Carolina before becoming pastor of Cofer's Chapel FWB Church in Nashville, Tennessee, a position he held from 1964 - 1981. He joined FWB International Missions where he was the Associate Director and then Director, until he retired in 1998. As the Director of International Missions, Mr. Waddell traveled to more than 40 countries, ministering to both the unchurched and the churched, and to the missionaries who called him their pastor. During his tenure the Mission began ministering in Russia, Mongolia, China, and Central Asia. Under his leadership contact with Cuba was reinstated, 64 missionaries were appointed, overseas church attendance almost doubled, and the TEAM summer missions program for high school students was initiated. In addition to his time as general Director, Waddell served as Associate Director for five years (1981-1986) and completed over 20 years (1959-1981) as an active member of the Board of Free Will Baptist Foreign Missions. Following his December 31, 1998, retirement, he served as Minister of Care and, more recently, Pastor Emeritus at Cofer's Chapel FWB Church in Nashville, Tennessee. Waddell leaves behind an impressive legacy of faith, love, and resilience, passion for reaching unreached peoples, integrity, compassion, mediation, vision and servanthood. Mr. Waddell earned a B.A. from FWBBC in Nashville and a M.A. from Columbia (SC) International University.

Clarence Wayne Wagner

Birth:
Jan. 22, 1936
Stigler
Haskell County, Oklahoma
Death:
May 9, 2014
Nolensville
Williamson County, Tennessee
Burial:
Nolensville Cemetery Nolensville
Williamson County
Tennessee

Reverend Clarence "Wayne" Wagner was the son of Clarence Wagner and Katie (--) Wagner. He was married about 1958 to Maxine -- . Wayne was a Free Will Baptist pastor and had preached for 55-plus years and his last position was with Heads Free Will Baptist Church in Cedar Hill, Tennessee. A resident of Nolensville, Wayne was 78 years old when he passed away.

John L. Welch

Birth:
Unknown
Death:
Jul. 24, 1988
Nashville,
Davidson County, Tennessee
Burial:
Spring Hill Cemetery,
Nashville,
Davidson County,
Tennessee

He had early influence in both conferences of the East and West, and had much to do in bringing them together as a denomination in 1935. The meeting was held at the Cofer's Chapel Free Will Baptist Church where he pastored. Reverend Welch was the first moderator of the National Association of Free Will Baptists in 1935. He also had influence in the beginning the Free Will Baptist Bible College to Nashville, Tennessee., and served 12 years as a member of the college's Board of Trustees, and pastored Cofer's Chapel Free Will Baptist Church in Nashville 53 years.

Mrs. Mary Welch served faithfully as a secretary at the college, spent nearly 60 years as a pastor's wife, and was a leader in the women's movement. For the past five decades, there has been a building on campus named in honor of John and Mary Welch — the historic Welch Library. He was 94-years-old at the time of his death. Free Will Baptist Bible College in 2012 renamed the school Welch College in their honor.

WELCH, Rev. John L— Sunday morning July 24, 1983 at a local infirmary. Age 94 years. Survived by daughter, Mrs. William M. (Jean) Henderson, Joplin, Mo.; daughter-in--law, Mrs. Bessie Welch Smalley; four grandchildren; eleven great grandchildren. His remains are at the Eastland Chapel, 904 Gallatin Road. The remains will lie in state at the Cofer's Chapel Free Will Baptist Church, 4300 Clarksville Highway Tuesday afternoon from 1 until time of services at 2 p.m. with the Pastor Billy Gene Outland, Dr. Robert E. Picirrille, Rev. R. Eugene Waddell, Rev. Henry Oliver, and Dr. D. Michael Henderson officiating. Interment Spring Hill Cemetery. Honorary Pallbearers: Ministers of Cumberland Association, Free Will Baptist Headquarters, and Free Will Baptist Bible College. Active: Bill Smith, Jimmie Carter, Seybert Basford, Jack Trotter, Jack Nicholson, John Boyte, Willie Owen, Jarman Goodman, and Webb Cofer. IN LIEU OF FLOWERS, MAKE CONTRIBUTIONS TO COFER'S CHAPEL FREE WILL BAPTIST CHURCH OR TO THE FREE WILL BAPTIST BIBLE COLLEGE. ROESCH PATTON DORRIS & CHARLTON, Eastland Chapel, 904 Gallatin Road, 244-6480

Rev Jerry Wayne Whitworth
Birth:
Jun. 2, 1951
Springfield
Robertson County, Tennessee
Death:
Apr. 12, 2005
Nashville
Davidson County, Tennessee,
Burial:
Heads Free Will Baptist Church
Cemetery
Cedar Hill
Robertson County, Tennessee

The Rev. Whitworth was owner of Old Stuff Antiques and a member of Pardue Memorial Free Will Baptist Church. He was a minister at Christian Home Free Will Baptist Church in Blountstown, FL, Second Free Will Baptist Church in Ashland City, KY, and director of Cumberland Camp in Clarksville, TN. He was a member of the Montgomery County Historical Society, the Middle Tennessee Genealogical Society, and a charter member of the Cheatham County Art Guild.

Funeral services were held at Heads Free Will Baptist Church in Cedar Hill, TN, with Brothers Len Scott and David Williford officiating.

Juna J Wilkerson
Birth:
Jun. 2, 1910
Death:
Dec. 19, 1994
Burial:
Carters Chapel Cemetery,
Greene County, Tennessee

Dr Jack L Williams
Birth:
1942
West Carroll Parish
Louisiana
Death:
Apr. 29, 2016
Antioch
Davidson County
Tennessee,
Burial:
Cremated

Dr. Jack Williams, former editor of Contact magazine, died Friday, April 29, 2016, at age 73. Jack had struggled to regain his health since November 2012, when a massive stroke left him partially paralyzed. Jack was born in 1942 on a sharecropper's cotton farm in West Carroll Parish, Louisiana. He was saved in 1958 at age 16 at nearby Sardis Free Will Baptist Church. Eight months later he accepted God's call to preach. When the Sardis Church offered him a pastorate shortly thereafter, the 17-year-old high school senior accepted, and using a borrowed Bible, began his nearly 60-year ministry.

After graduating from high school, Jack attended Free Will Baptist Bible College, graduating in 1966 with Bachelor of Arts and Bachelor of Theology degrees. More importantly, he met and married Janis Wilcox, "prettiest girl in West Virginia," as he called her. He continued his education at Sacramento Baptist Theological Seminary, completing a M.A. in 1973 and a Ph.D. from Louisiana Baptist University in 1976.

From 1959-1969, Jack pastored churches in Louisiana, Tennessee, and Arkansas, before accepting a position as academic dean at California Christian College, where he remained for eight years. Then, in 1977, Jack began what became his life's work as editor of Contact magazine and executive assistant for the Free Will Baptist Executive Office. In addition to editing the magazine, the role included oversight of day-to-day operations and the planning of the annual convention.

Jack quickly earned a reputation for excellence and professionalism, both in the convention planning community and in the publishing world. He was named Meeting Planner of the Year by the Association for Convention Operations in 1995 and received the President's Award from the Religious Conference Management Association in 2001.

He was known for witty writing, journalistic objectivity, and constant encouragement and development of new writers. His strong journalistic ethics are evident in the words of his final Contact magazine editorial: "Those who wield the journalistic sword must be careful where they lay the edge of the blade lest they harm the innocent while probing for truth." His writing and work as editor earned 13 awards from the Evangelical Press Association and helped launch a fleet of new Free Will Baptist writers.

In 2005, after Contact magazine ceased publication, Jack accepted a position as director of publications for Welch College, where he remained until his retirement in 2014. Provost Greg Ketteman reflected on Jack's time at the school: "He arrived on campus early each day and maintained an open-door office policy welcoming students, faculty, staff, and visitors. He did an excellent job preparing news releases, editing publications, and fulfilling other duties as communications director."

Throughout his life and ministry, Jack remained fully dedicated to the work of Free Will Baptists. In addition to a number of local and regional positions, he served as assistant moderator of the California State Association (1971-1977), member of the national Sunday School Board (1975-1977), and chairman of the Free Will Baptist Press Association (1978-1991). Another notable denominational work was with the Free Will Baptist Historical Commission, where he served from 1977 until his passing.

Robert E. Picirilli recalls his long-time friend: "Jack was one of the good guys, a personal friend whom I admired. Nobody loved the Free Will Baptist denomination and its ministries any better. He was a gifted speaker and writer, spoke positively about others, and believed in building up rather than tearing down. We'll remember him most for his long stint as editor of Contact, and I for the many years we worked together on the FWB Historical Commission. We will miss him."

Executive Secretary Keith Burden noted, "Jack Williams was an encourager, a cheerleader. He may have been short in stature, but he cast a long shadow across our denomination. I'm a better leader and writer because of Brother Jack."

Perhaps the best way to remember Jack is to recall his own words, penned in an editorial for Contact magazine: "The point of all this is that the work of God goes on when the people of God die. Abraham dies—Isaac steps up. Moses dies—Joshua leads Israel across Jordan. Stephen dies in the last verse of Acts 7. Acts 8 opens with God's hand already on a young man named Saul of Tarsus. The work of God never stops. The people of God wipe away the tears, strap on their spurs, and keep looking up...I like the way God writes obituaries for His people. They all end, not with a period, but with a comma."

Jack is survived by Janis Wilcox Williams, his wife of 53 years; daughter, Dr. Rebecca Deel and husband Recardo; son, Brad Williams and wife, Tina; grandchildren, Austin Deel, Andrew Deel, Kristen Williams and Kullen Williams; sister, Carol Mariche; and brother, Jerry Williams. He was preceded in death by a grandson, Kyler Williams.

Funeral services was held Wednesday, May 4, 2016, 7:00 p.m., Woodbine Funeral Home, His grandson, Becky's son, Andrew Deel, gave the eulogy and then he read the obituary which he said Jack wrote a few years back. Jack's pastor, Steve Marcum of the FWB

church in LaVergne, TN brought the message.

Homer Emerson Willis
Birth:
May 8, 1924
Clintwood,
Dickenson County, Virginia
Death:
Feb. 17, 2005
Nashville,
Davidson County, Tennessee
Burial:
Woodlawn Memorial Park,
Nashville,
Davidson County, Tennessee

A Free Will Baptist pastor, evangelist and denominational leader. He was converted to Christ at age 15 and ordained to the ministry at age 18. He graduated from Free Will Baptist Bible College in Nashville, Tennessee in 1946 and also Trinity College. He pastored churches in Michigan, Tennessee, Kentucky and North Carolina. He was General Director of the

National Home Mission Board of Free Will Baptists from 1956 until 1973. During his tenure the department planted churches in 33 states and he opened the work in Canada, the Virgin Islands, Puerto Rico, and extended the work in several states of Mexico. He was founder and editor of *Mission Grams*, the Director Of Evangelism, founder of the Church Loan Fund Program and the Director of the Chaplain's Ministry. He preached in all 50 states and Canada, Mexico, Puerto Rico, the Virgin Islands, Germany, Israel and Egypt. His ministry took him to every continent except Australia. He was an honorary life member of the Gideon's, a past Lieutenant Governor of Kiwanis International, an organization that he had served for 50 years. He was a member of the Who's Who in Tennessee.

Rev Caleb Winters
Birth:
1760
Death:
Feb. 18, 1843
Adams
Robertson County, Tennessee
Burial:
Heads Free Will Baptist Church
Cemetery
Cedar Hill
Robertson County, Tennessee

Rev. Caleb Winters is said to have been a charter member of Heads FWB Church, in 1840. His dau., Elizabeth, married Rev. Geo. Head,

(1760-1843) who donated the land for Heads church and cemetery on of Moses Winters and Elizabeth Head.

Large monument in cemetery lists children and spouses. Occupation was Baptist Minister. He was one of the first settlers in this part of Tennessee. Came to TN with his father in 1779. Father of 21 children total. Four born after he turned 75.

About 1781 Caleb settled on a farm in Robertson County. It is said that he subsisted entirely upon meat during the first season.

From *"Goodspeed's History of Robertson County, TN"*
About 1781 Caleb Winters settled on the farm now owned by Hon. G. A. Washington. It is said that he, like Kilgore, subsisted entirely upon meat during the first season.

Caleb Winters was a pioneer Baptist Preacher. He came with the first settlers in 1779, he lived in a cave on Caleb's Creek the first year, and was a citizen of Robertson County for over 60 years. Parents: Moses Winters (1732 - 1798) & Elizabeth Head Crain Winters (1737 - 1815). Spouses: Mary Duncan Winters (____ - 1852) & Sarah Harris Winters (1765 - 1826).

Rev Clayton Ballard Wolfenbarger
Birth:
Oct. 23, 1904
Bryson Mountain
Claiborne County, Tennessee
Death:
Oct. 19, 1946
Fonde
Bell County, Kentucky
Burial:
Cedar Grove Cemetery
Cedar Grove
Knox County, Tennessee

Clayton Ballard Wolfenbarger, 42 of Fonde, KY, was a minister of the gospel. He was married to Mrs. Lula Mitchell Wolfenbarger, of Fonde, KY; The funeral service,was in the Free Will Baptist Church in Fonde, KY, with the Rev. Billie Moyers and Rev. Ben Bowman officiating.

Paul H. Woolsey
Birth:
Nov. 23, 1908
Death:
Jun. 19, 1989
Burial:
Burial:
Harris Memorial Cemetery
Greene County
Tennessee

Rev. and Mrs. Paul Woolsey were tremendously interested in the educational system of the county in East Tennessee. Woolsey served on the Greene County Board of Education for six years, two of which he was chairman of the board and one year due to the sickness of the superintendent, most of the work of that office fell to him. When he accepted the call to the mission field, he and Mrs. Woolsey were teaching in the elementary school of Cedar Creek, formerly the Cedar Creek Presbyterian Academy.

Rev. and Mrs. Woolsey worked in the local church and continued their visits in the interests of the entire work of the denomination during the year and a half that they were in the community. They not only supported the school in every possible way, but contributed liberally to their equipment fund for India.

They left America from New York City April 10, 1947 and arrived in Bombay Monday on May 5. They proceeded to Kotagiri, Nilgiris, South India and joined Miss Barnard in her labors there during the hot season. In the month of July, they entered the Language School at Landour, Mussoorie, in the United Provinces of North India, preparatory to the opening of a new work in North India. Turbulent India, about to gain her complete independence, is a long way from the peaceful home where the family had dwelt since the days of the independence of the United States. Much of the history of the Woolsey family can be found in the book he wrote entitled, *"God, A Hundred Years and a Free Will Baptist Family."*

William B. Woolsey
Birth:
May 19, 1821
Greene County, North Carolina
Death:
Feb. 10, 1905
North Carolina
Burial:
Harrison Cemetery, Greystone,
Greene County, Tennessee

He was converted at the age of 21 yrs and joined the Nebo Baptist Church. He soon felt his calling to further endeavors and began to preach, being licensed in 1843. However, his strong views on Arminism vs Calvinism, saw a break and along with two other older talented ministers, Moses Peterson and John Wheeler, they withdrew and formed the Toe River Association of Free Will Baptists with six churches, scattered between the mountains. William Bonaparte was elected clerk and remained so for eighteen years. By 1854, they had twelve ministers and more churches. He, though not afforded a formal education, began at once to study, buy Bible helps, and classics, as he could, and soon rose to a place of leadership among the people. He knew the value of education, sought it himself, and promoted it for others. He was self-educated and had a wise head about him. He, and others, established the Woolsey College, going far and near to try to secure funds or support, to build it, which they did, so that the youth could attend school and have some training after the devastation suffered by the Civil War. He organized Horse Creek Church in 1849; assisted in organizing Dry Fork FWB; and Nebo. He lived an active life in the ministry and raised a large family who followed his footsteps. (*"My Free Will Baptist Woolsey Family"*, by Rev. Paul H. Woolsey, pub 1949" a great-grandson.)

Rev Jonathan Garth Yandell
BIRTH
30 Oct 1958
Oklahoma City, Oklahoma County, Oklahoma, USA
DEATH
20 Jun 2019 (aged 60)
Nashville, Davidson County, Tennessee, USA
BURIAL
Woodlawn Memorial Park and Mausoleum
Nashville, Davidson County, Tennessee, USA

Rev. Jonathan G. Yandell, 60, Antioch, passed away on Thurs. June 20, 2019. Jonathan was an ordained minister, and always as a young lad wanted to be 'a preacher' and writer. He graduated from Hillsdale College, Moore, OK (now Randall Univ) and served as youth minister at Trinity FWB, OKC, church while attending college there. He married Dianna Redfearn, a student, and later they worked as a Home Missionaries in Sacramento, CA, and afterward, as Pastor at Garden Grove Free Will Baptist Church, in the L.A. Calif. area. It was from this pastorate he was hired by Randall House Publications in Nashville, Tenn., and became Senior Editor for Adult SS literature, from 2003 to 2016. He was diagnosed with MS before this assignment and battled it until his death. He wrote "Finding Hope in the Darkness. He was a member

of The Donelson Fellowship in
Nashville, and taught in the Sunday
School Dept.